Tuning Your British Sports Car

by
CHARLES WILLIAMS

DRAKE PUBLISHERS   NEW YORK

ISBN 87749–165–8

*629.1
W67t

Published in 1972 by
DRAKE PUBLISHERS INC
381 Park Avenue South
New York, N.Y. 10016

73 23

Printed in Great Britain

CONTENTS

ILLUSTRATIONS

INTRODUCTION

To most people, a 'performance' car is one that goes faster than usual. While it is true that all performance cars are fast cars, this is only part of the overall picture. For in addition to eager engines, these cars need superb brakes and above average road-holding to handle the power that they have.

Fortunately it is not necessary to purchase a small but expensive sports car to enjoy above-average performance. Most small family cars can be modified to perform better after a number of minor engine alterations and perhaps some attention to the brakes and suspension. The precise treatment required depends on the car involved, and it can usually be carried out in several stages, stage one being the mildest and most inexpensive stage of tune.

To most people there is an air of mystery surrounding the work tuning experts do to make ordinary cars go faster, and this is possibly because theirs is a business that breeds trade secrets. The aim of this book is to part the veil a little and give a reasonably non-technical, but practical, guide to how family cars can be made to behave a little more like sports cars.

Among the converted, there are two attitudes to a modified car.

The 'wolf in sheep's clothing' group prefer their high powered car to be anonymous and only distinguishable from its brothers and sisters by its performance. The other approach is to modify the outside of the car as well, and towards the end of the book there is a chapter on customizing showing how fiberglass can give a vehicle new identity.

American owners of British-made cars will have no difficulty in obtaining the British products mentioned in this book from American dealers in foreign auto parts, and the book includes a list of major US suppliers of these parts.

LIST OF US SUPPLIERS OF FOREIGN AUTO PARTS

ALLIED FOREIGN CAR PARTS
73-22 Northern Boulevard
Jackson Heights, New York 11372

AUTO WORLD INC.
701 N. Keyser Avenue
Scranton, PA. 18508

ECONOMY IMPORTS
287 Tyler Avenue
San Jose, California 95117

FALCON BROTHERS
51 Charles Street
Mineola, L.I., New York

FOREIGN AUTO PARTS
14860 E. Whittier Road
Whittier, California 90605

GLOBE FOREIGN AUTO PARTS INC.
646 Coney Island Avenue
Brooklyn, New York

IMPORTED PARTS WEST
2535 East Colorado Boulevard
Pasadena, California 91107

INTERNATIONAL CAR PARTS
7109 Reseda Boulevard
Reseda, California 91335

J. C. WHITNEY & CO.
1900 South State Street
Chicago, Illinois 60616

1

THE STANDARD ITEM

The only reason people modify cars is because they are dissatisfied with their standard performance. But often a car is not giving even standard performance because a certain amount of neglect has allowed it to 'run down'. Perhaps the valve gaps are wrong, the spark plugs may be overdue for renewal, the brakes soggy, the dampers soft and the suspension and steering loose at the joints.

A vehicle in this state is not worth modifying until its basic ills have been cured and it has been brought up to standard condition. Quite frequently, after this has been done, the driver changes his mind about going any further. So before laying a spanner on your car in the interests of extra performance, make a number of checks so that you do begin with what is truly the standard item.

First, take a long hard look at the car and ask yourself: 'Is it worth it?' A tired ten-year-old family saloon half eaten away by rust underneath is best left alone. On the other hand, a car that has been regularly serviced and is in clean condition bodily can be modified almost regardless of age.

Corrosion Even if you think your car is rust-free, just to be on the safe side it is worth making a check on some vital areas underneath before you decide to go ahead with any modifications. The points to look at are places such as the suspension mounting points and sections of the chassis that hold important items like the steering-box or rack.

On cars using strut-type independent front suspension, for instance, there is a tendency for the dirt thrown up by the front wheel to collect at the mounting point where the strut is fixed to the bodyshell. Once dirt has collected here, every time it rains it soaks up water like a sponge and retains it at the mounting point long after the wet roads have dried out. The end product of this continuous wet poultice is corrosion of the strut mounting. On some cars this has culminated in the strut breaking through the bonnet-top when the rusty metal finally gives way.

Similarly, at the rear, some cars with leaf-type springs have a rust trap near the front mounting points. Corrosion here can only be spotted by occasional checks underneath. Once again, if it is left, the spring can force its way through the floor-pan.

A number of cars nowadays use separate sub-frames which carry the engine and front suspension. And some have two sub-frames, the back one carrying the rear suspension. Of the two, it is the rear sub-frame that is most liable to corrosion—engines almost inevitably spread a film of oil around the front one—and if the corrosion becomes serious, the car's handling is affected as the suspension mountings twist. Fortunately, sub-frames are relatively cheap and can be renewed if this happens.

Hidden corrosion is easy to find. All you need is an $\frac{1}{8}$in screw-driver to prod at suspect metal. Thick flakes of rust indicate that the area is seriously weakened, and the only real cure then is to have the bad metal cut away and a 'patch' of new metal welded in its place.

Most body repair specialists can do this work for you—although a lot of them prefer not to. They have valid reasons for this attitude: welding on to rusty metal is tricky—they cannot *guarantee* the strength of the repair and they usually

have more than enough work doing accident repairs on nearly
new cars, anyway. Some body repairers, however, can be per-
suaded to get out the welding torch if you offer to do the
donkey-work yourself. This means you would cut out the new
patch, remove all the weak metal, and present the car with the
patch held in position with blind rivets or self-tapping screws,
so that all the body-builder has to do is run a torch round it.
But he is still unlikely to guarantee the repair.

A car that needs a lot of patching-up is liable to be lethal if it
is modified to perform better. So if in doubt, before doing anything, run it round to the local body-repair shop and be guided
by the professionals.

Tyres Tyres, like corrosion, can be a bit depressing. They are at
their best when almost new, but from this point they wear out
and there is nothing that can be done to improve them. The
only cure for a worn-out or faulty one is to buy a new cover.
Unfortunately, if you are contemplating working them a little
harder, you must apply higher standards to them than would be
needed, say, for the tyres on a milk float. So begin by examining
the tread. In Britain, the law decrees that it should be at least
1mm in depth all the way round and across three-quarters of its
width, but in practice this is getting a bit thin for fast motoring
and it is wiser to renew tyres when the tread depth is nearing 2mm.

Originally, when tubeless tyres were first fitted to cars, there
was a good deal of publicity given to the fact that a puncture
could be repaired without taking the tyre off the wheel—you
simply inserted a plug of rubber dipped in rubber solution into
the hole. But there have been instances of these plugs coming
out, so that plug repairs on tubeless tyres are now only recommended as a temporary measure. To make the repair permanent, the tyre must be removed from the wheel, the spare 'tail'
of the plug inside the tyre cut off flush, and a patch vulcanised
over it. When selecting tyres for a modified car, it is particularly
important to make sure that any repairs have been given this
treatment. Similarly, radial tyres with bulges in the side-walls

should not be used until you have had them checked and cleared for high-speed use by a tyre specialist.

The pattern of tyre tread wear can tell you a lot about the car's suspension. For instance, a tyre that has its tread 'feathered' towards the outside of the wheel is running with too much toe-out. If the feathering is towards the inside of the wheel, the toe-in is too great. Both these conditions affect the steering and the handling of the car in a corner. A further undesirable side-effect is that the tyres will wear out more quickly. You can get a rough and ready idea of the front wheel alignment using planks or stretched strings resting against the sidewalls of the tyres, although the only real way to do the job is with a tracking gauge. Virtually all garages have one and make only a modest charge for tracking the front wheels.

Suspension The quickest way to check for wear in the suspension is to adopt the method that motor sport scrutineers use on competition cars. They grip the top of the tyre and push and pull it sideways as if they are trying to wrench the wheel off the car. This sort of treatment will quickly show up any play in the suspension—usually the worn item will be heard knocking and can often be felt at the wheel.

There will be other signs, too. On the road, a car with something loose or worn in the suspension or steering will let you know in one way or another. Worn wheel bearings, for instance, will rumble or whine on smooth roads. Depending on which bearing is affected, the noise will alter on corners and this can be used to locate the bearing. Normally, a faulty bearing quietens down if the wheel is pressed towards the car. This means that a bearing on the left of the car (from the driver's seat) will quieten down on right-hand corners, and become noisier on left-handers. As a double check, the car should be blocked up and the tyre gripped top and bottom and rocked gently sideways. Ideally, there should be just perceptible play at the wheel rim, and when the wheel is turned the bearing should run quietly. If it clicks or rumbles, it needs renewal.

The average car has two bearings per wheel, and normally it is necessary to use a special puller to draw off the hub, after which the bearings, which are often an interference fit, are removed from the hub. This can be done either by drawing them out using one of the manufacturers' special tools or, if this is possible, by driving them out with a hammer and a drift. New bearings must be fitted with the thrust face the correct way round (make a note when the old bearings come out) and must be entered squarely. The best method of entering them into the hub is initially to press them in using a large vice, after which a piece of pipe the same diameter as the outer cage can be used—again with the vice—to press the bearing up against its housing in the hub. If you do not have a large enough bench vice, it is possible to tap the outer cage into the hub using a hammer and drift, but it is important to tap all round the perimeter of the outer cage to avoid distortion.

Swivels The hinge on which the sub-axle pivots when the wheel is turned to take a car round a corner was once known as a king-pin. Nowadays, ball-joints or swivels may be used, depending on the type of front suspension. On the road, worn swivels will betray their presence by knocking when the car is being driven over bumpy surfaces. The best way of double-checking is to have a helper rock the top of the tyre sideways with the car standing on its wheels, while you check the suspension for unwanted movement.

On cars which still use king-pins—the MG Midget for example—it is normal for the softer king-pin bushes to wear before the hardened steel pin. So, on this type of layout, it could be that all you need is a set of new bushes.

Before you go to work, check in the workshop manual whether it is necessary to compress or remove the road-spring. In most cars it is not, but there are exceptions, and special equipment may be needed.

On the double-wishbone suspension system used on the Midget, the bottom wishbone is jacked up well inboard of the king-pin pivot, after which work can start. Once the king-pin assembly has been removed, you will come up against a snag— the new bushes will not fit the old pin. This is because they are made undersize and must be reamed out after they have been fitted to the stub-axle assembly so that they fit the king-pin exactly.

The sort of reamers needed are sometimes available for hire. If you cannot obtain them, it is often possible to keep the labour charge down by arranging for a garage with the appropriate equipment to fit the new bushes and ream them after you have done the work of getting the stub-axle and old king-pin out.

Cars using strut-type front suspension, like most of the Ford range, have one ball-swivel at the bottom and at the top the

Fig 1

All suspension pivots should be checked for excess free play. The arrows show the places to look at if a car has strut-type front suspension strut pivots on a bearing. If the bottom joint needs renewal, this can be done without any need to compress the spring—during dismantling, the ball-joint is simply levered away from the bottom of the strut using a long length of timber to press the track control arm down.

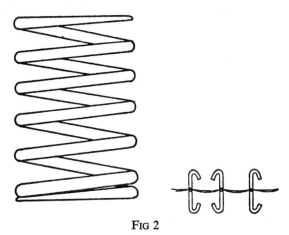

FIG 2

Holding a road spring compressed requires spring keeps. On the Ford Anglia the keeps should embrace at least four coils. As a general rule, try to restrain at least half the coils

But if the upper bearing needs renewal, you will need three spring keeps. On the 105E Anglia, for instance, these are made from $\frac{3}{8}$in mild steel bar with a hook bent at each end, the distance between the internal bend of the hooks being $4\frac{3}{4}$in. Get two or three friends to sit on the wing of the car and compress the spring, then slip the three keeps over the spring so that each embraces four or five coils. Tie them round the outside with wire to ensure they cannot slip out. You can then release the strut at the top and dismantle the upper mounting without fear of the spring shooting out as soon as the upper nut is released. Incidentally, the dimensions for the spring keeps given for the Anglia will need to be varied on other cars and reference should be made to the workshop manual.

The rear suspension system on the average British small car

B

is reasonably uncomplicated in that the majority use a one-piece live axle. Where this is suspended on leaf springs, the individual leaves should be checked edge-on for breakages and excess wear, which can be caused by the end of a short leaf bearing against a larger one and wearing it thin.

On cars with live axles and coil springs, the linkage that locates the axle fore-and-aft and sideways should be checked for excess wear at the pivot points. These are generally rubber bushes and when they are worn the damage is easy to spot.

On independent rear suspension systems, use the same method of checking for free play as on the front. Most of the joints will be rubber-bushed, but in some cases—the Triumph Spitfire and Herald, for example—nylon bushes may be used. Where these are renewed, it is important to fit correctly the dirt shields provided with each set of new bushes.

Dampers Soft dampers will allow the car to wallow on bends and undulating surfaces, giving the driver uncertain control of the vehicle. Fortunately, dampers can be quickly checked without climbing under the car. All you do is get one corner of the car bouncing healthily and let go. The bouncing should continue for $1\frac{1}{2}$ movements, at which time the dampers should have ironed out the body movement.

If the car keeps bouncing after two rebounds, check the damper body just by looking at it. Normally, one that is working half-heartedly has sprung a leak and is perhaps only half-full of fluid. On dampers that can be topped-up, much of the performance will be restored by topping-up with the correct shock-absorber fluid. But leaking dampers cannot be repaired, so sooner or later it will pump out all its fluid again. The only remedy is a new damper, and as a general rule they should be fitted only in pairs, since a new one on one side of the car and an old one on the other can give different handling on left- and right-hand corners.

Steering Does the car wander when you meet a join-line in the road or if you edge a front wheel against a raised white line? If so, the chances are that there is a lot of unnecessary play in the steering linkage, and the most common place for this to happen is at the ball-joints. These may or may not be used throughout the steering linkage, but are certainly used where the track-rod ends connect to the steering arms on the stub axles.

You need a helper to turn the steering wheel back and forth while you check the steering linkage, either by watching or feeling for movement at the ball-joints. Most of these joints are of the 'sealed for life' type, and not designed to be further lubricated. This means that once they have failed they must be renewed. The method of attaching the joints to a steering track-rod is to screw the socket to the threaded end of the track-rod, while the pin which connects the ball to, say, the steering arm, has a taper which is pulled up tight by a nut on the end of the pin. Undoing the nut is easy, but breaking the taper can present a problem and most manufacturers provide their dealers with special clamps or wedges to use to break the taper joint. If you do not have any of this special equipment, the best substitute is a pair of big hammers.

With the nut off, place one hammer behind the eye on the steering arm and hit the opposite side of the eye with the other hammer. A good hard clout is generally sufficient to jar the taper free. If this does not work, do not try hitting the end of the pin to free it, you will only damage the threads and so be unable to re-fit the nut in case, as a last resort, you have to run the car round to the local garage for them to do the job.

Where the ball-joint is fitted to one of the steering rods, it is locked by a nut on the thread. It is important when removing the old joint to count the number of turns screwed on to the thread and to do up the new joint exactly the same number of turns when fitting it. This will avoid altering the tracking of the vehicle when the job is completed.

One or two of the stodgier family saloons use rubber-bushed joints in the steering linkage, and where these have become impregnated with oil they allow some free play to develop in the

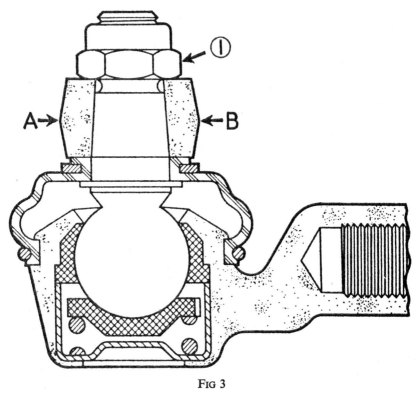

FIG 3

A typical steering ball-joint. To break the taper, undo nut (1) place a heavy hammer on one side of the steering arm eye (A) and hit the opposite side (B) with a 2lb hammer

system. Such bushes should be renewed, and if you are unable to stop oil from contaminating them, taping some polythene sheet round them will keep the oil away.

Another possible cause of slackness, or a hit-or-miss feeling in the steering, is a loose steering box or rack and pinion unit. The remedy is obvious.

Brakes Braking has a complete chapter to itself further on, where most of the more common brake faults and remedies are dealt with, so here we will restrict ourselves to testing the brakes.

Pick an empty stretch of dry road that is fairly level and has a firm surface. Motor up to 20mph, select neutral, make sure that there's nothing behind, and put the brakes on hard. Ideally, the car should stop very smartly in a straight line with some squeal from the tyres. It should not pull to one side. If it does, repeat the test, just in case one of the wheels hit a slippery patch of gravel.

Brakes that are 100 per cent efficient will pull a car up from 20mph in 13·4ft. Unfortunately, 100 per cent efficiency depends a great deal on ideal weather conditions and road surface, and because of this most car manufacturers are reasonably happy with a consistent 85 per cent braking efficiency, which represents a stopping distance of 15·8ft from 20mph or 35·5ft from 30mph. Assuming the linings and/or disc pads on your car are in good condition, these figures should easily be achieved.

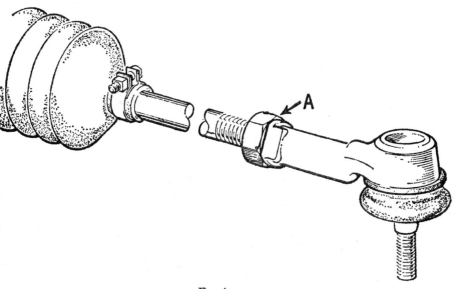

FIG 4

When renewing steering joints, after loosening the locknut (A) wind it back to its original position. This allows the old joint to be removed and the new joint fitted in the same position on the steering track rod and avoids re-tracking

If repeated tests show the car to be pulling to one side, check the front tyre pressures, since one soft tyre will pull the car off line during heavy braking. If a soft tyre is not causing the deviation, there are a number of other possibilities, depending on the braking layout, and these are covered in Chapter 3.

Engine The best guide to the condition of an engine is its fuel and oil consumption. A standard Mini that does, say, 20mpg and gets through a pint of oil every sixty miles is obviously suffering from something. And if it is not leaking fuel and oil in large quantities, the chances are that it is so worn out that engine tuning will only bring the day of total collapse a little nearer.

If, however, the fuel consumption and oil thirst are within reasonable limits for the engine, make a visual check. Take a critical look at the exterior of the engine. It should be free from oil from leaking gaskets. It is a bad sign if blue smoke pours from the crankcase breather pipe when it is revved-up, since this suggests that there is a lot of blow-by past the pistons due to worn rings or bores.

The water hoses should be in good shape. Most people do not replace hoses until they burst, with the result that a lot of five-year-old cars have hoses that are hard with age or puffed-up to twice their normal size because they have broken down inside. If they are in this state any slight extra load that a modified engine may put on the cooling system will cause one to burst.

If the car has an oil-pressure gauge, the reading should be within the manufacturer's recommendations at 50mph in top gear after the engine has covered about ten miles. Low oil pressure is normally blamed on worn crankshaft bearings or a worn oil pump, although it can also be caused by an oil-pressure relief valve that has jammed or has a weak spring, a partially blocked oil filter element, or oil that has over-heated because of a spell of continuous high-speed running.

Although it can be argued that competition engines are normally assembled so that the clearances are on the loose side to minimise friction, it would be unwise to modify a standard engine with poor oil pressure, since the extra power output will put a greater load on the crankshaft bearings. The same argument applies if the clutch slips when it is engaged, or if there is excessive judder—although in this case, before condemning the clutch, check the engine mountings, for if these are very soft they will cause judder. If the engine passes this stage, the next step is to check the adjustments.

The handbook or workshop manual will state whether the valve gaps should be set hot or cold, and on overhead-valve engines these should be measured with a feeler-gauge and reset to the standard settings if necessary. On some overhead camshaft engines, such as the Hillman Imp or Rover 2000, valve adjustment involves removing the camshaft and quite a bit of arithmetic as shims of varying thicknesses are placed under the bucket tappets to alter the valve gaps. On these cars I would be inclined to ignore the valve clearances at this stage and take comfort from the fact that they only normally require adjustment at major overhaul intervals. Fortunately, the other adjustments—checking the plug gaps, points gap and setting the timing—apply to all petrol engines.

Spark-plug manufacturers recommend that a new set of plugs be fitted every 10,000 miles or so. The reason is that an old plug has a higher voltage requirement than a new one, and at high revs there is a chance of misfiring. If you are not sure of the age of the plugs, you can check a worn one after it has been removed from the engine by examining the electrodes. In time these erode away, the centre electrode gradually becoming dome-shaped at the end, and a corresponding indentation forming in the side electrode immediately above it. When this happens, the voltage requirement of the plug goes up so that a heavier high-tension pulse is required to persuade the spark to jump from the centre electrode to the side electrode.

When the plug is new, the end of the centre electrode is flat and the sparks normally jump from the sharp edge. Up to a point, this can be achieved on an old plug by filing the dome-shaped centre electrode flat, flattening out the side electrode immediately above it and resetting the gap. But sooner or later you will run out of electrodes, and new plugs will be needed. And certainly, if you are after peak performance from the engine, it is not worth making do with old plugs.

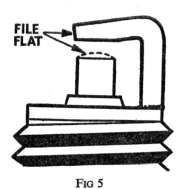

FIG 5

Spark-plug life can be extended a little if the electrodes
of worn plugs are filed flat

The contact-breaker points in the distributor are reasonably critical so far as gapping is concerned, since the wrong gap can advance or retard the ignition timing, as well as making starting difficult. After fitting new points it is not unusual for the gap to close up perhaps ·005in during the first 500 miles as the fibre or nylon heel which bears on the distributor cam wears a little.

On coil ignition systems it is normal for the slight arcing between the points to build up a pile on one contact and a corresponding pit on the other. The interlocking action of these two surfaces can give a false reading when the gap is measured with a feeler gauge, and in the interests of accuracy, if the points have been in use for more than about 3,000 miles, it is wise to remove them and use an oilstone to remove the pile from one contact. The pit can be left in the other. It is important to stone the contact squarely, so that an accurate gap can be measured when it is replaced. If you are not familiar with removing and replacing contact breaker points, make a note of the positions of the various insulating washers as they come out since assembling them in the wrong order will mean that the engine will not start.

After the points have been set, the ignition timing can be checked. Most cars have a notch or mark on their crankshaft pulley which is aligned with an adjacent pointer. The pointer is sometimes a multiple one indicating when no 1 piston is at top

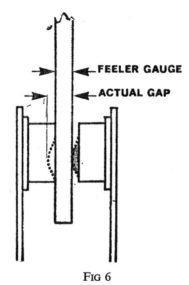

FIG 6

Pitting and piling on contact-breaker points gives a false feeler-gauge reading which in turn will affect the ignition timing. The pile should be filed flat before setting the gap

dead centre, 5 degrees before and maybe 10 degrees and 15 degrees BTDC as well. If we assume that the manufacturer's recommended ignition timing is 5 degrees BTDC, this is in-dicated when the ignition points *just* begin to open as the notch on the pulley is adjacent to the 5-degree pointer.

To show accurately when the points open, it is customary to wire a 12v bulb between the contact breaker terminal on the side of the distributor and earth. The bulb will light the instant the contacts separate. Before checking the timing, make sure the automatic advance and retard mechanism is free by turning the rotor arm in its direction of rotation. If all is well it will spring back.

Timing is checked with the plugs out and the ignition on. It is usually easiest to put the car in top gear and pull it slowly forward on a level surface, stopping the moment the test bulb lights. The relative position of the pulley notch and the pointer can then be noted. Small adjustments are made by turning the vernier scale on the side of the distributor where one is fitted, or by slackening the distributor body and turning it in the same direction of rotation as the rotor arm to retard the ignition and vice-versa to advance it.

Some cars, such as the Mini, have their timing marks on the flywheel. On this car a small cover is removed from the clutch housing and the flywheel marks and the adjacent pointer on the clutch housing are viewed with the help of a mirror.

Once all the adjustments have been made, examine the carburettor air cleaner for blockage, and if it is serviceable, set the carburettor as detailed in Chapter 7. The car may then be road-tested as described in the same chapter to establish a set of standard performance figures. These will provide the basis for comparisons when the engine has been modified.

2
ROADHOLDING AND HANDLING

A car's roadholding could be expressed as the maximum speed at which it can safely be driven round a given corner. The handling describes the manner in which it behaves on the way round. On a car where more power than normal is being extracted from the engine, it may be desirable to have better roadholding and improved handling to match.

To a motor manufacturer, the way a saloon car handles and sits on the road is something of a compromise. One of the reasons for this is that the average motorist values comfort and a soft ride more highly than predictable handling. As a rule, he never drives near the cornering limit and so the finer points of roadholding do not interest him. The easy way for a car manufacturer to provide a soft ride is to fit the vehicle with soft springs. But the soft-spring solution is complicated by the fact that the loading on quite a small car can vary from the driver only aboard to a full-load condition which may include five adults, a boot-full of luggage and some overspill on a roof-rack. With this load, soft springs would compress to the bump-stops, so a stiffer spring is used—still as soft as possible—and combined with a reasonable travel to avoid bottoming under full load.

27

Although our average driver does not want to corner very fast, he still likes to feel confident in the vehicle, so, in addition, the car must have a predictable 'feel' to it to give this confidence. All in all, it sounds an impossible formula to keep to, but somehow the average British car manages to combine all these features, and within its designed speed range it holds the road and handles pretty well. So, for small power increases such as those detailed in Chapter 4, the chances are that no alterations at all will be needed.

Some of the more popular methods of modification are dealt with later but, before deciding which alterations are needed, it is a good idea to examine the way the car handles in standard form. Some of the more common handling traits are as follows:

Roll The amount a car rolls is dictated by its centre of gravity and suspension geometry and stiffness. Cars which roll the most are usually those with soft springing and a long travel. A car that rolls excessively is uncomfortable and a little more difficult to control on twisty roads than a car with a firmer ride.

On a few cars, a lot of body roll can cause a phenomenon known as 'roll-oversteer', which comes to light when negotiating S-bends. What happens is that the weight transfer from one side of the car to the other causes roll which makes the suspension linkage steer the rear wheels a little. This can be due to incorrect suspension geometry, though it is more likely to be caused by the compliance of the rubber bushes in the suspension linkages. The result is that the car feels decidedly unpredictable from the driver's seat. A close relative to roll-oversteer is 'bump-steer', which means what it says—bumpy surfaces (which cause large suspension movements on certain suspension layouts) can steer the car, causing the vehicle to dart from side to side. This can also be quite unnerving.

Understeer and Oversteer As a rule, car manufacturers build their vehicles to understeer. An understeering car tends to run wide when cornered hard and extra steering lock is required to keep to the desired line. Backing-off the accelerator when the car is under-steering has the effect of pointing the nose of the vehicle into the bend and tightening the line.

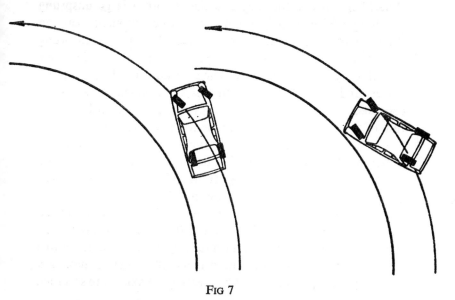

FIG 7

Understeering cars (*left*) need extra steering lock to pull them round a corner. An oversteering car tends to slide its tail outwards near its cornering limit

The opposite condition is oversteer. Oversteering cars have a tendency to slide the tail outwards when cornered hard and this can be corrected by paying off a little steering lock. In practice, the steering on a car that oversteers is more sensitive, and the average driver seldom reaches the point where correction is needed—except perhaps inadvertently on a sharp, slow corner. The reason car manufacturers prefer understeer is because it is the easier to correct by the natural reactions of putting on more steering lock and backing off the throttle. There is an added advantage that the extra lock causes front tyre scrub which slows the car down. An oversteering car, on the other hand, does not slow down appreciably when the steering correction is applied. It also needs more room for correction than an understeering car.

Wheel-hop This is normally associated with a large unsprung weight and fairly high-output engines. All components between the road spring and the road surface add up to the unsprung weight, and on a rear-wheel-drive car with a one-piece live axle this means the complete rear axle unit, the hubs, brakes, wheels and tyres. If a car with this arrangement is being accelerated fairly briskly over a bumpy road, the upward momentum of the wheels and axle may be too much for the springs to keep them in contact with the ground, so wheel-hop develops. If the power is held on the situation often gets worse, for the wheels will spin each time they lift off and this will result in even more axle movement as they rise and fall.

Axle tramp, which also brings on wheel-hop, is caused by a leaf-sprung live axle winding-up and then being 'unwound' by the springs. This normally occurs only when a considerable amount of power is fed to the driving wheels when making a standing start. It can be cured by locating the axle more securely.

FIG 8: SUSPENSION SYSTEMS

Front:
STRUT: Popular at the front of Fords, the strut acts as a king-pin as well as coping with spring and damping. An anti-roll bar (see Fig 1) connects both front units

WISHBONE: A lower wishbone with an upper link connected to a lever-type damper is used on some BLMC cars. An alternative is to use upper and lower wishbones with a telescopic damper inside the coil spring

SWING AXLE: Only occasionally used at the front, this set-up is fitted on the Hillman Imp range. Wheel camber alters directly in relation to axle movement

Rear:
LIVE AXLE: Simple, the only non-independent system shown here, it has the advantage of keeping both wheels vertical. It has a high unsprung weight

SWING AXLE: A cut-price independent rear layout which, if it is allowed large angles of positive and negative camber, can give unpredictable handling at high cornering speeds

TRAILING ARM: A fairly sophisticated rear layout, it requires double-jointed drive-shafts and generally gives predictable handling with a good ride

Fig 8   SUSPENSION SYSTEMS

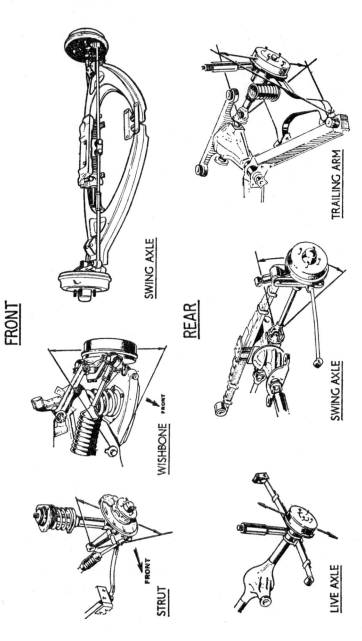

FRONT

SWING AXLE

WISHBONE

FRONT

STRUT

FRONT

REAR

TRAILING ARM

SWING AXLE

LIVE AXLE

If your car suffers from an overdose of any of the above handling peculiarities, it is generally possible to make an improvement. We will begin in the most logical way and work from the ground up.

Tyres For road use there is the choice of two types of tyre, radial and cross-ply. The names refer to the construction of the tyre carcass.

Radial tyres have two laminations of fabric cords in the side-walls and the direction these run in is radially—that is at 90 degrees to the tread from bead to bead. Under the tread of the tyre there will be several more bracing layers of fabric and on some tyres a woven steel stiffener as well.

Cross-ply tyres may have four or more layers of fabric and the direction of the cords is diagonal in relation to the tread, and on alternate layers they go in the opposite direction and cross-over. There are the same number of casing plies in the sidewalls as there are under the tread.

So, in a nutshell, a radial tyre can be described as having a very tough tread supported by pliable side-walls, whereas a cross-ply tyre has an overall stiffness about it with much more rigid sidewalls. Bearing in mind the fact that racing tyres are always of cross-ply construction, it would seem that these are best for fast road use. But this is rarely so. Most modern cars stick to the road better on radials. The reason for this is that the soft walls of the radial deform more where the tyre rests on the road, and allow more tread to 'unwrap' than the cross-ply. Broadly speaking, the more rubber you can put on the road, the more grip you will get.

The radial is even more impressive when it is rolling. The extra bracing under the tread discourages any deformation, with the result that most of the tread rubber stays flat on the road. Even during harsh cornering, the extra bracing keeps the tread flat and it begins to lose its grip only when the flexible sidewalls have allowed the wheel rim to overhang the tread as the car is pushed by centrifugal force towards the outside of the corner.

C

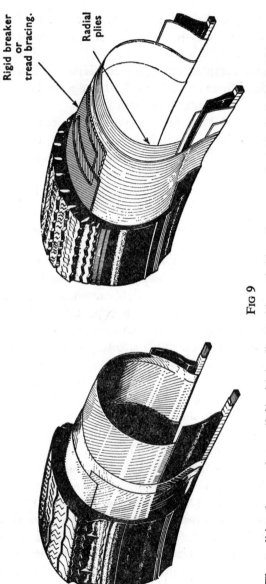

Rigid breaker or tread bracing.

Radial plies

Fig 9

The traditional cross-ply tyre (*left*) with its diagonal-braced sidewalls compared with a typical radial-ply tyre with a strongly-braced tread and flexible radially-braced sidewalls

Cross-ply tyres behave differently. The stiffer sidewalls have a great influence on the tread and do not allow it to unwrap such a large contact patch on the road. Pressed hard through a corner, the complete tyre will bend sideways under the action of centrifugal force and eventually the edge of the tread nearest the inside of the corner will begin to lift.

If you are driving fast, a tyre's behaviour at breakaway point—the instant that it begins to slide—becomes very important. As a rule, cross-ply tyres give the car a much more predictable feel at the point where a slide begins and the gentle breakaway characteristics are the main reason for adopting this construction for racing tyres since drivers exploit this, generally aiming to take corners very close to the tyre's breakaway point.

Although radial-ply tyres generally hold the road a little better, when breakaway point arrives it comes more quickly than with a cross-ply. Some early examples of radial-ply tyres were notorious for their sudden unpredictable breakaway on wet roads. Happily this has been corrected to some extent and although most radials still breakaway quite quickly, they do give the driver some warning—usually by a lightening of the steering—so that corrective action can be taken in time.

Earlier it was mentioned that radials suited modern cars best. This does not mean that they cannot be used on older cars, but it must be realised that some early models, particularly high-performance ones, had their handling tailored to the more gentle breakaway of cross-ply tyres and radials could make them a bit more tricky near the limit.

There is also the question of noise. The heavier bracing of the radial tread makes more noise over road joins and cat's-eyes, and the thin sidewalls allow more tyre vibration. On an old suspension design this can result in an uncomfortable amount of road noise being transmitted to the chassis. In cases of doubt, consult the car manufacturer or a tyre maker. On cars where radial tyres are a standard fitment or are offered as an option, the road noise problem is reduced as much as possible by design-

ing the suspension with generous-size rubber bushes which do
not transmit so much noise and vibration.

One subject that tyre manufacturers do not discuss much in
regard to radial tyres is radial roll-over. It has already been
pointed out that the flexibility of the sidewalls allows the wheel to
overhang the tyre tread when cornering hard. Now assume that
the car is being driven very quickly through an S-bend. At the
point where the steering is changed from one lock to the other,
the overhanging wheel will come back over the tyre and then
overhang the other side. This is radial roll-over and from the
driving seat it feels like a certain amount of lost motion. It
varies according to the car and the width of the wheel rims and,
once experienced, can be allowed for. But if you are not
familiar with radials and contemplate high speeds, it pays to
feather the car gently into the corners at first until you get the
feel of them.

On a performance car, the mixing of radial and cross-ply
tyres is not to be recommended, since the handling characteristics of both tyres are different. If mixing tyres is unavoidable,
the radials *must* go on the back and the cross-ply tyres on the
front—this applies regardless of whether the car is front- or
rear-wheel drive. If textile and wire-braced radials are mixed,
the wire-braced ones go on the back wheels, and if 'town-and-
country' type radials and road-going radials are mixed, the
'town-and-country' pattern go on the driving wheels. Cross-ply
and radial tyres should never be mixed on a common axle. The
same applies to fabric- and wire-braced tyres.

Racing tyres are sometimes seen on the road, usually on fun
cars such as Beach Buggies. Unfortunately, they do not perform well off the circuit, mainly because racing tyre development has reached the stage where drivers can select one with
the appropriate tread compound for wet or dry track conditions. So unless you are willing to do an all-round wheel change
every time the weather alters, there will be occasions when your
racing tyres are a bit down on roadholding.

Understandably, racing tyres are built as light as possible

and this means that only the thinnest covering of rubber is used on the sidewalls, so inadvertent kerbing can wreck one. If that is not enough to put you off, it is worth remembering that racing tyres are designed to work best when the road wheel is upright. Volkswagen-based Beach Buggies have swing-axle rear suspension which allows the back wheels to make large camber changes, and the grip given by the racing tyres will vary with the camber. In practice, these tyres also give an extremely bumpy ride. The reason Beach Buggy drivers put up with racing tyres is, I suppose, because the tyres are very wide and give the vehicle an aura of power (in fact few VW Buggies can exceed 70mph). A face-saving compromise would be to swap the racing tyres and wheels for a set of 7in rims—which are still fairly wide— shod with something like the Dunlop E70 VR 15 SP Sport radial used on the Jaguar XJ6. The roadholding will be im- proved tremendously.

Modern radial tyres include the letters SR, HR or VR on their sidewalls to denote the recommended maximum speed at which the tyre should be operated. Tyres marked SR can be used at speeds up to 113mph, HR radials are suitable for speeds up to 130mph and VR are suitable for speeds in excess of 130mph.

It is customary to increase the tyre pressures if a car is being driven continuously at high speeds. Goodyear recommend that for continuous running at 100mph on their radials, pressures should be increased by 6psi all round, with an all-round increase of 12psi for speeds up to 125mph. Dunlop do not make any overall suggestions, but agree with the principle that tyre pressures on both cross-ply and radial tyres should be increased for high-speed running, since it reduces sidewall flexing and discourages overheating. For slower speed work, the normal tyre pressures should be used, since over-inflation will cause the centre of the tread to wear out first.

Altering tyre pressures will change a car's handling characteris- tics. Increasing the inflation pressure improves a tyre's road- holding, and racing drivers often use this to slightly alter the handling of a car to suit a particular circuit. On a car with a lot of understeer, for instance, putting up the front tyre pressures will improve the roadholding of the front wheels and reduce the understeer. It will also make the steering more precise. Similarly, with an oversteering car, increasing the rear tyre pressures will discourage the tendency to slide the tail.

Experiments with inflation pressure differentials are best done on a closed circuit and can be useful if the car is used for weekend competition work. Increased pressures cannot really be recommended for road use since a big increase will cause rapid wear. There is, of course, a limit to the amount of pressure increase, for—depending upon the bumpiness of the surface— sooner or later you reach the stage where the tyres begin to jump off the ground and the car becomes skittish.

Tyre rotation is a subject on which the major tyre companies disagree. Some suggest changing all the wheels round at, say, 3,000-mile intervals in order to bring the spare into use and equalise tyre wear. Others, particularly where radials are concerned, say they should be left on the same corner of the car all the time and renewed in pairs when the front or rear tyres wear. There are arguments for both sides, but with radials it is often found that the pattern of tread wear on the front wheels is completely different to the wear pattern on the rear, and changing these over can cause handling problems. Bearing in mind that front tyres frequently wear out before the rear ones, I am inclined to renew the two front tyres when they get down to 2mm of tread, and renew the rear ones when they get to the same stage. At least this means that only two tyres are bought at a time. If the wear is evened out by regular wheel rotation, you are eventually stuck with a bill for five new tyres all at once.

Wheel Balancing This was once regarded as a fetish of the favoured few who owned performance cars. Nowadays, with motorways within the reach of most motorists in the Western world, balancing of at least the front wheels is rightfully regarded as a major contribution to smooth motoring.

The symptom of a car with out-of-balance front wheels is a

tremor which afflicts the steering at around a certain speed—
say 50mph. Often the shaking goes away if the car is speeded
up perhaps 10mph, but returns as the speed drops within the
critical range. If it is ignored, the tyre will not only wear (the
heavy section will wear more quickly than the remainder of the
tread) but the twisting, tramping action of the wheel will
accelerate wear on the wheel bearings, suspension bushes and
swivels or king-pins.

There are two methods of wheel balancing, the most popular
being to balance the wheel and tyre assembly off the car statically
and dynamically. The other method involves the same balancing
operations, only the job is done on the car. Of the two methods,
on-the-car balancing is the best, but the more inconvenient. It
is best because besides the wheel and tyre, the brake drum or
disc and the hub assembly are balanced at the same time. Badly
out-of-balance hubs and brakes are rare, admittedly, but they
are not unknown and, where they occur, on-the-car wheel
balancing is the only method of curing the trouble. The disadvantage is that once a wheel has been balanced on a hub, it
must always be fitted to that hub, in the same stud-holes or on
the same splines to avoid upsetting the balance. So, if you are
in the habit of rotating the wheels on the car to bring the spare
into service, you must either break the habit or have the front
wheels re-balanced each time.

Dampers By the law of logical progression, after tyres we should
move to wheels. However, I have brought forward the section on
dampers because a change of dampers all round can often have
much more effect on a car's handling than the fitting of wider-
rim wheels.

The first step towards transforming a softly-sprung, roll-prone
family car into a machine with the taut, instant response that a
fast car needs is to control the rate of roll. In particular, it is
important to iron out any tendency for the car to lurch as
weight is transferred when going from one steering lock to the
other. Also, it is most desirable on cars that suffer from axle-

tramp or wheel-lifting on acute bends to ensure that all wheels stay on the ground as much as possible.

A change to dampers with harder settings can sometimes achieve all this and often is the only modification that a road car needs to make it handle better. Dampers with 20–25 per cent harder settings are readily available, and have the advantage that they provide a more responsive feel without making the ride unduly firm. Of course, stiffer dampers cannot alter the *total* amount that the vehicle rolls, since this is dependent upon suspension geometry, spring stiffness and the centre of gravity, so on a long fast corner even if you fit very firm competition-type dampers, the car will eventually reach its original roll angle. But the stiffer dampers will make sure it gets to the full roll position more slowly, and for shorter corners there will not be sufficient time for the car to get to full roll.

The effect of strong dampers on axle-tramp depends to some extent on the mounting position of the damper. Where a damper is mounted vertically or, better still, is inclined forwards from its mounting on a live rear axle, fitting stiffer units will have a material effect on tramp and wheel hop. The effect will be less where the dampers are inclined at a steep angle towards the centre-line of the car, as on the Ford Escort, for instance. In general terms, though, anything which discourages rapid rising and falling or twisting of a live rear axle will keep the back wheels on the ground.

In the same way as tyre pressures, dampers with different settings front and rear can also alter a car's handling. Softer settings at the front encourage understeer, while soft settings at the rear will cause a tendency to oversteer, and the availability of adjustable dampers means that in theory you can 'tune' a car's suspension to your own tastes. Adjustable units are available for most cars using telescopic or strut-type dampers as standard equipment, although at the time of writing there are no adjustable units to replace lever-type dampers where the damper forms the mounting point for the front suspension upper wishbone. This system is used on a number of BLMC cars.

Experiments by *Practical Motorist* with a set of Armstrong 'Adjustaride 22' dampers fitted to a lightweight Ginetta G4 sports car confirmed that adjustment can have a startling effect on a car's handling. As the name suggests, 'Adjustarides' have twenty-two different settings normally covering the range from one click softer than standard to twenty settings harder. But on the test units, standard damping was provided with setting no 10 selected. Four tests were made to check the effect of various settings on the car's handling. In standard form, the vehicle understeered on the entry to a corner.

Test 1: All dampers wound to their softest setting. Result: a soft ride on the straights, but cornering produced an excessive amount of roll, the car tended to wallow on bumpy corners, and individual wheels hopped off the ground. Steering became unresponsive and the car still understeered.

Test 2: All dampers wound to their hardest setting. Result: every bump was transmitted to the chassis, the vehicle rattled constantly, and even on moderately bumpy corners there was a tendency for both back wheels to leave the ground at times. There was more cornering power than with Test 1, but the car still understeered. Steering was very responsive, but road shocks were transmitted to the wheel. The quick steering meant that the throttle could be used to kick the tail out and produce a condition close to a four-wheel slide round right corners, although constant correction was needed over the bumps.

Test 3: Front dampers at their softest setting, rear dampers at their hardest setting. Result: a noticeable increase in the degree of understeer coupled with an expensive amount of tyre scrub. In corners, the car took up a pronounced nose-down attitude as the front tried to roll more than the rear. Steering unresponsive, some snaking during heavy braking.

Test 4: The reverse of Test 3, front dampers on their hardest setting, rear dampers in the fully soft adjustment. Result: unpredictable handling under all conditions. On straights, the car pitched violently at speeds around 90mph, while on bumpy corners it would change direction without warning, as the tail-end did a sort of fish-tail action. Since the behaviour was so peculiar, it was difficult accurately to assess the degree of understeer. The general opinion was that possibly it had diminished, although that which had replaced it was far worse.

The ideal compromise on this car was with the front dampers set on no 12 and the rear ones on no 14. This gave a slightly stiffer ride than normal, but with enough resilience to deal with bumpy surfaces without excessive wheel-hop or the whole car leaping sideways on corners. Steering response was good, but without too many road shocks being transmitted to the wheel. The understeer was about the same as normal.

The above tests illustrate that very hard shock absorbers not only give an uncomfortable ride and put considerable strain on the body chassis unit, but can also hamper the traction available in corners by perhaps allowing the complete back end of the car to lift off the road after it has hit a bump. It is interesting that the final settings coincide roughly with the 20–25 per cent increased stiffness which most shock-absorber manufacturers recommend as the optimum for road cars.

There are some cars where switching standard dampers for stiffer ones is not possible. On BLMC cars with Hydrolastic 'float on fluid' suspension, for instance, there are no external shock absorbers. Damping is catered for by valves inside the Hydrolastic displacer units. Fortunately, Hydrolastic suspension has good built-in anti-roll qualities, although there is a tendency for the car to pitch over undulating surfaces. This can be reduced by fitting external telescopic dampers at the front, or by enlarging the bump-stops so that these come into operation much earlier.

Wide Wheels The benefits to be gained from the fitting of wide-rim wheels are fairly obvious. A wider rim allows more rubber to be put on the road with a consequent improvement in roadholding in the dry. Because it provides a wider base for the tyre to sit on, there is liable to be less tyre flexing and handling is likely to be improved on twisty roads. If the wheels increase

Fig 10

'Hydrolastic' suspension as used on some BLMC cars has good built-in anti-roll properties but is not always so good at self-levelling as these diagrams suggest. On some surfaces it can pitch a lot—a condition improved by fitting bigger rear bump-stops

the track of the vehicle, this would seem to discourage any tendency for it to roll over.

Most small British saloons use wheels with rim widths between $3\frac{1}{2}$in and $4\frac{1}{2}$in. On cars with the smaller rim widths in particular, increasing the width by an inch will give a meaningful improvement in roadholding—the general rule-of-thumb seems to be in the region of 10 per cent. For small increases like this it is usually possible to retain the same tyre size. Thus, a Mini

which as optional equipment uses a 145 × 10 radial tyre on its
3½in rims can retain the same tyre size on a 4½in wheel. But this
is *not* an infallible rule and it is advisable to be guided by the
tyre makers or the wheel manufacturers if in doubt.

If you stick to small increases in width, you will avoid most
of the wide-wheel pitfalls. Most cars can accept an extra inch
in width without any modification to the wheel arches to prevent
them being clouted by the fatter tyre profile. Again, this is not
an infallible rule, and in cases of doubt it is a good idea to cram
as many friends as you can in and on the car and (if you can)
tape-measure the clearance between the inside and outside walls
of the tyre and the nearest point on the body or chassis. Pay
particular attention to items such as brake pipes and shock
absorbers. At the front, take measurements with the wheels on
full left and right lock.

Armed with these measurements you should be in a position
to decide whether you want wide wheels with offset or inset.
An offset wheel is one where the extra rim width is put on the
outside edge, so to speak, so that the track of the car is increased
a little. An inset rim has the extra width on the inside of the
wheel. In theory, it is preferable for the extra width of the wheel
to be accommodated equally on both sides of the rim, since
this puts the centre-point of the tyre tread in the same place
and the suspension geometry and the load on the wheel bearings
are not changed.

In practice, however, this is not always possible. On the
standard Mini, for example, any extra inset on the rear wheels
makes the tyre touch the radius arm, so any extra width must
be brought about by increased offset. This in turn puts a slightly
greater load on the wheel bearings. BLMC get over this problem
on the Cooper 'S', which has 4½in wheels as standard, by fitting
heavier-duty wheel bearings and building out the drums so that,
in effect, they incorporate spacers to bring the wheel mounting
further away from the inside of the wheel arch.

Now, if you wanted to fit Cooper 'S' wide wheels to a Mini,
spacers would be required between the wheel and standard

brake drum to prevent the inside of the tyre hitting the radius arm. In fact, it is possible to buy alternative wide wheels from British Leyland with the appropriate amount of offset so that they bolt on to the Mini without the need for spacers.

Earlier, reference was made to the pitfalls of very wide wheels. Broadly speaking, there are two problems—mechanical and legal. The mechanical problem of fitting, say, 7in wide wheels to a Ford Escort is that there is insufficient room to get the wheel in the wheel arch without fouling the bodywork. On the Escort and some other saloons, the rear wheel arch is a double-skinned load-bearing section so it is not possible simply to cut metal away. If you did, putting it crudely, as soon as you drove over a bump the boot would fall off.

So any modification here has to be strong. Ford Motor Company produce a wheel arch extension kit for the car which contains flared wheel arch extensions pressed from sheet steel. To fit them, the double skin of the arch is cut away and the new metal spot-welded in position. After blending in the edges with filler, the car is re-sprayed. As one might guess, it is an expensive job.

The legal problem is that regulations require that the bodywork should cover the wheels above a horizontal line passing through the hub. We have seen what this involves on the Escort but, fortunately, not all cars are as difficult. On the Mini, for instance, the wheels are always clear of the edge of the wheel arch. So if 4½in wheels or wider are being fitted, the car can be made legal by fitting a set of glass-fibre wheel arch extensions, using a few self-tapping screws. British Leyland Special Tuning can supply extension kits for 4½ and 5½in wheels. They have been designed so that even the original wheel arch trim can still be used.

If you are running on wider-than-normal wheels, the assumption is that the car is a lot more powerful than standard and the extra-wide tyres are there to provide extra traction. Up to a point, this is a logical argument. But with wheels that are too wide you reach the stage where standing starts put a big shock-load on the transmission, and eventually gearboxes or perhaps half-shafts begin to break with monotonous regularity. With a slightly narrower wheel, the safety-valve of a little wheelspin as the clutch engages takes a lot of load off the transmission. Most ultra-wide wheels are made to order. Where they are made from steel, the extra width may be obtained by cutting the outside edge off the standard wheel, welding a band of steel on to the wheel, and then welding the original edge on to this band. Providing the welding is properly carried out and the wheel is accurately made, the final result should be as strong as a similar one made with a one-piece rim. It is extremely difficult to tell the quality of welding by looking at it, particularly if it has been ground and painted. But, for what it is worth, it always pays to examine the welds on this type of wheel if they are being purchased, and to reject any where the welding looks very irregular.

Some porosity of the welding is normal with this construction and it is customary to fit tyres with tubes. Where steel wheels only one or two sizes wider than standard are being produced for road use, they are generally made in greater quantities and usually have a one-piece rim.

So far, it has been assumed that the wide wheels are made of steel. These are the cheapest, but they are, of course, heavier than the narrower wheels they replace, and increase the unsprung weight of the vehicle. The weight penalty can be avoided if the standard steel wheels are replaced by aluminium wheels which, even with wide rims, are a little lighter in weight. These are twice or three times the price of wide steel wheels, which is their main snag, although to their credit they usually improve the appearance of the car as well as the roadholding. The ultimate in wide wheels is the magnesium racing wheel which is exceptionally light, very rigid, but a little fragile if run up against a kerb. I would not recommend them unless a car was doubling as a road and track car, and they are usually around twice the price of a comparable aluminium wheel.

Summing-up the wheel situation, assuming you are only

contemplating increasing the width by about an inch, the chances are that, providing you get wheels designed for your car, there should be no fitting problems. You will probably be able to use the existing tyres, and there will be immediate benefits to the handling.

With the improved handling, the 'feel' of the car is likely to change a little. The steering will almost certainly be a trifle heavier at slow speeds, and if the wheels have offset rims it is likely that the steering will lose a little of its self-centring action and may feel a little more 'dead' in the straight-ahead position. On the other hand, the steering will feel more precise when cornering.

Camber Changes When a car is cornering, it is preferable if the tyre remains more-or-less upright, or that the camber of the wheel stays as constant as possible. Unfortunately, on cars with swing-axle suspension this is not possible because the working of the suspension automatically changes the wheel camber angle.

Among the more popular cars with swing-axle rear suspension are the Triumph Herald and Spitfire, early Vitesses and GT6s and a large number of VW Beetles. When one of these cars is laden, the rear wheels take up a negative camber angle. Looked at from the rear, the wheels are angled with the tops of the tyres nearest the centre line of the car, as if they formed the sides of a letter 'A'.

If one of these cars is cornered hard, as it rolls, and centrifugal force acts on the outside wheel, there is a tendency for the rear suspension to jack up. When this happens, the camber changes from negative to positive (as if the wheels were aligned with a letter 'V') and this causes the rear track to decrease. The effect of all this is to move the tyre tread relative to the road surface, and at high cornering forces it can unstick the back end and cause a slide or spin. A further side-effect is that, with a lightly laden car, there will be even more positive camber, and on very severe corners there is a possibility that the inside rear

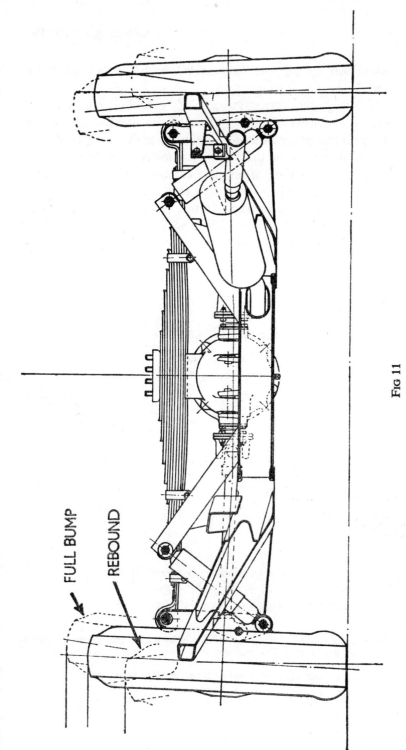

FULL BUMP

REBOUND

Fig 11

Triumph Herald swing-axle rear suspension. Total wheel camber change between full bump and full rebound is 18 degrees

wheel will lift off and the outside wheel will tuck under the vehicle, causing it to overturn.

The way most suspension specialists tackle swing axles is to limit the amount of camber change from negative to positive. They do this either by fitting a reset rear spring or by modifying the existing set-up so that the car sits lower at the back, and the wheels are in a state of negative camber even when the car is unladen. The result is that the wheel must travel downwards— or the body of the car go up—further before it can change to the more unstable positive camber condition. If stiffer rear shock absorbers are also fitted, wheel movement is further controlled and stability improves considerably.

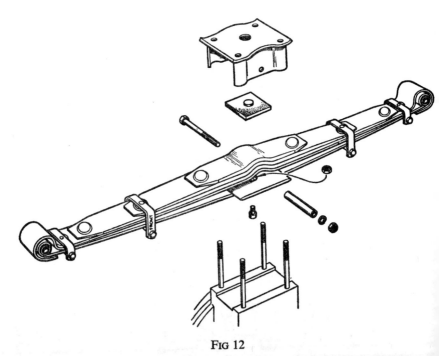

FIG 12

All but the bottom leaf on the Spitfire Mk4 transverse spring are free to pivot at the centre. The reduced roll stiffness improves handling and cornering power. This arrangement can be transferred to earlier Spitfires. The Mk4 front anti-roll bar should also be used

Page 49 (*above*) Customised Mini. Instructions for modifying the bonnet-top to take the extra lamps are given in Chapter 8; (*below*) Saturday morning GT. It takes less than an hour to fit this GT hard-top to a Sprite or Midget. Perspex roof panels brighten the interior

Page 50 (*top*) How *not* to use an aerosol. The operator's finger is overhanging the button, interrupting the spray and producing blobs of paint; (*centre*) spray too close and the paint builds up too quickly and runs like this; (*bottom*) too far away and the paint spread is uneven because it partially dries en route

A popular way of modifying the rear suspension of the Triumph Herald and Vitesse swing-axle cars is by removing the transverse leaf spring, dismantling it and reversing the no 4 leaf (counting from the main leaf). The locating dimples must be ground off when this is done. This modification gives about 2 degrees of negative camber with the car unladen.

On the Triumph Spitfire, Standard-Triumph has improved matters on the Mk4 version by pivoting all but the main leaf of the rear spring at its mounting above the differential. This reduces rear roll stiffness and the wheels tend to take up a negative camber attitude when cornering. The Mk4 also has a stiffer anti-roll bar at the front. This and the modified rear spring and its mounting can be fitted to earlier Spitfires.

For those who do not relish a lot of dismantling, a bolt-on swing-axle improver is a camber compensator. This is an extra transverse leaf spring which links the rear suspension uprights and is pivoted at its centre point. It discourages the suspension from changing to high degrees of positive camber and at the same time keeps the inside wheel on the ground.

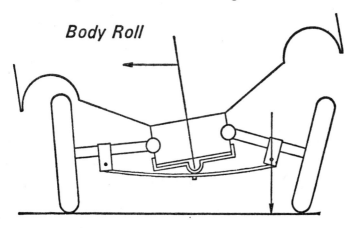

Body Roll

Right-Hand Bend

Fig 13

Speedwell camber compensator

D

The Hillman Imp also uses swing-axle suspension, but on this car the swing axles are at the front and their effect on the handling is not so marked. Early models had pronounced positive camber at the front in the unladen state and handling could be improved by fitting shorter springs front and rear, which at the front gave a more-or-less vertical wheel when unladen. An alternative approach at the front was to lower the axle pivots to give slight negative camber. Negative camber should only be added to the front wheels in small amounts since excessive negative camber at the front on cars which were not designed to take it can cause the vehicle to dart from side to side on straight roads where the surface is uneven. On the Imp, the steering rack should be repositioned when the pivots are lowered, otherwise there will be excessive kick-back at the wheel.

On cars without swing axles, where the amount of camber change is less, adding some negative camber generally improves a wheel's cornering power since the tyre can 'dig in' more. This principle is used by a motorcyclist when he cranks his machine over on fast bends.

On some road cars, adding a little negative camber to the front wheels is used to correct excessive understeer. Such a modification involves either lengthening the bottom wishbone or transverse link, moving the pivot point outwards a small amount, or fitting a new suspension cross-member. This modification will almost certainly affect the feel of the steering, possibly making it heavier, perhaps taking away some of the self-centring action, and maybe transmitting more road shocks to the wheel. For the road, it is what I would call a borderline modification, and is not really necessary on most road cars unless they double as competition vehicles.

Anti-roll Bar This does what its name implies. Mostly fitted at the front, it is a steel torsion-bar that connects the stub-axle assemblies of both wheels on an independent layout. It is free to swivel in its mountings on the chassis so that it does not affect the rate of the suspension when both wheels are equally loaded.

But when the car rolls, the bar resists the upward movement of the outside wheel and discourages roll. At the front an anti-roll bar increases the amount of understeer. At the rear it encourages oversteer.

Lowering Certainly the most obvious suspension modification, lowering brings down the car's centre of gravity, so reducing roll. But bearing in mind that most road-going cars occasionally are driven over rough surfaces, the amount the average car can be lowered is limited to about 1–1½in, depending on the standard ground clearance.

The method used varies with the car. Vehicles with leaf springs and live rear axles can be lowered by having the springs re-set to a flatter profile. A bolt-on alternative to this is to interpose lowering blocks between the spring and axle, using longer U-bolts. The only snag with this method is that, on fairly powerful cars, moving the axle away from the spring increases the risk of axle-tramp. This can be minimised by fitting anti-tramp bars, as we shall see later.

At the front, cars with coil springs can be lowered a small amount by fitting alternative springs. Stiffer springs with a

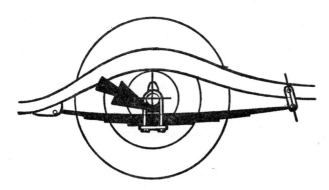

FIG 14

Cars with leaf-sprung live rear axles can be lowered by using longer U-bolts and sandwiching lowering blocks between the springs and axle casing

different rate from standard should be used, not simply shortened versions of the standard spring as with these there is danger of the car continually coming down on the bump-stops.

On cars with strut-type front suspension, such as most Fords and the Rootes Arrow range, the standard struts can normally accept without further modification a spring which will lower the ride height up to one inch. Where the vehicle is being lowered more than this the rebound stop-tube inside the strut—which prevents the strut from over-extending itself when the front of the car rises—may have to be modified. This is because, on full rebound, there is a chance that a very short spring might not fully fill the gap between the upper and lower mountings and might hop off its seat, cocking between the mountings when the car comes down on it.

BLMC cars with rubber or Hydrolastic suspension cannot be lowered by fitting alternative springs, although stiffer Hydrolastic displacers are available for Minis. Of these cars it is normally only Minis which seem to get the lowering treatment and this is done on rubber-sprung models by removing metal from the end of the spring struts front and rear where they bear up against the ball socket. Up to a maximum of 0·312in may be removed front and rear, although this maximum figure is generally only used for racing. When Minis are lowered, it is important that shorter shock-absorbers, available from British Leyland Special Tuning, are fitted to prevent the shock-absorber mountings being strained. The brake pipes must also be moved from the top of the rear suspension arms to prevent them hitting the bump stops.

On Hydrolastic cars the principle is the same, although the maximum that can be machined from the displacer pistons at the front is 0·2in and 0·3in from the rear struts. Bump and rebound stops should be modified at the same time.

Anti-tramp Bars These prevent a rigid axle from winding-up when engine output has been increased, and are available in kit form to suit most cars which are prone to tramp. The bar is

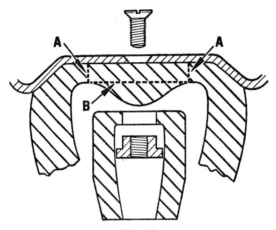

Fig 15

The big hollow rear bump-stops on the Austin Maxi can be stiffened by fitting an extra bump rubber in the centre. For road use, the existing rubber is cut away along the lines 'A', while for rally use the cut is made along line 'B', giving a harder ride and some oversteer tendencies

attached to the chassis at one end and to a mounting above or below the axle casing at the other. It is free to rise and fall with the suspension, but resists any attempts by the axle to twist. See Fig 16 overleaf.

Handling Improvements

The following list itemises some suggested 'Stage One' suspension alterations for a number of popular cars. Not all cars are listed because vehicles such as the Mini-Cooper 'S' or the Escort RS 1600 handle pretty well in standard form, so that further alterations only become necessary for competition work.

BLMC: The suspension systems split into two groups—Hydrolastic 'float on fluid' suspension, with its self-levelling action, self-contained dampers and first-class anti-roll properties—and cars using traditional steel springs, with independent front sus-

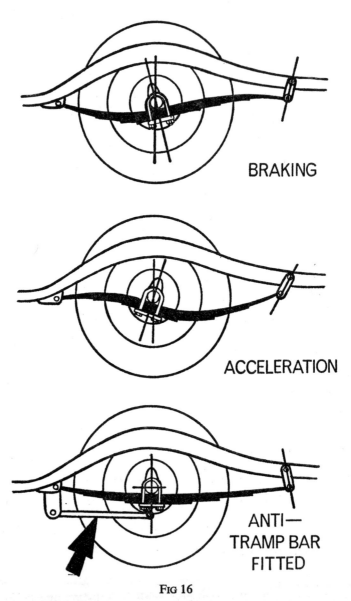

BRAKING

ACCELERATION

ANTI—
TRAMP BAR
FITTED

FIG 16

Anti-tramp bars discourage leaf-spring deformation and axle
wind-up during hard acceleration and harsh braking

pension and a live rear axle located on leaf springs. An exception to these is the early Mini which, until 1964, used rubber springs and separate telescopic dampers. The cars then switched to Hydrolastic suspension, but at the end of 1969, when BLMC fitted the wind-up windows, the Mini reverted to rubber springs. Rubber-sprung Minis are generally referred to as 'dry' cars.

Mini, Mini-Clubman ranges (including 'dry' cars but not Cooper 'S')	4½in or 5½in rim wheels, radial tyres
1100–1300 range	5in rim wheels, radial tyres.
Maxi 1500 and 1750	5½in rim wheels, radial tyres, modified rear bump stops.
1800	Modified rear bump stops. 5½in × 13in wheels (Mk2 cars use 4½in × 14in wheels as standard. These may not be readily available in 5½in rim widths. For improved cornering 5½in × 13in wheels can be used, but will lower the overall gearing and give more engine noise at high speeds).
Morris Minor, Austin Cambridge, and Morris Oxford series	Uprated dampers.
Sprite/Midget	Uprated dampers, 4½in or 5½in wheels, front anti-roll bar.
MGB	Uprated dampers, 5½in × 14in wheels, anti-roll bar.

Chrysler/Rootes: Three basic suspension layouts are used. The Hillman Imp range has independent suspension all round, using coil springs with swing axles at the front and trailing arms at the rear. The remainder of the cars have strut-type independent front suspension, although the rear suspension varies, the Avenger having a live rear axle located by four links, whereas the remainder have a live axle located by leaf springs.

Hillman Imp, Husky, Sunbeam Imp Sport, and Stiletto	Lowered front and rear springs to give approximately 1¼in lower ride height. Uprated front and rear dampers, radial tyres on standard 4in rims, although 5½in rims available if required.

| Hillman Avenger | Uprated dampers, 5½in rim wheels, radial tyres. |
| Hillman Hunter, Sunbeam Vogue, Alpine, Hillman Minx saloon and estate | Uprated front struts and stiffer rear dampers, 5½in rim wheels, radial tyres. |

Ford: All cars dealt with have strut-type independent front suspension and a leaf-sprung live rear axle.

Anglia 105E, Cortina Mk1 and 2, and Corsair	4½in rim wheels, radial tyres, front anti-roll bar, lowered front springs, lowered (reset) rear springs or lowering blocks and anti-tramp bars. Uprated struts and dampers.
Cortina GT and Corsair GT	5½in rim wheels, front anti-roll bar, uprated struts and dampers.
Escort 1100 and 1300	As Anglia 105E.
Escort GT	As Anglia but with 5½in × 12in wheels.
Capri 1300, 1600 and 2000	5½in rim wheels, radial tyres.

Standard-Triumph: Various suspension systems are used. They include the rather unsatisfactory all-independent system with coil springs and wishbones at the front and a transverse leaf spring and swing axles at the rear used on the Herald, Spitfires Mks1–3, early Vitesses and GT6s. Spitfires from the Mk4 model have an improved swing-axle layout, while later Vitesses and GT6s have double-wishbone rear suspension which reduces the wheel camber change. In addition, there is all-independent suspension on the front-wheel drive Triumph 1300, using coil springs and double wishbones at the front and coil-sprung radius arms at the rear. The Triumph 1500 and Toledo, which look very like the 1300 at first glance, also use independent coil-and-wishbone suspension at the front, but are non-independent at the back, the 1300 using a normal live axle and coil springs, while the 1500 has 'dead beam' axle and coil springs.

The TR range of sports cars changed suspension systems when the TR4A IRS was announced. Up to then they had used a coil spring and wishbone front layout and a live axle on leaf springs at the back. All models after the IRS version have independent rear suspension with trailing arms and double-jointed drive shafts. The Triumph 2000 has strut-type front suspension and a similar rear end layout to the independent TR models.

Swing rear axle cars: Herald/Spitfire Mks1, 2 and 3, early Vitesse and GT6	Reset rear spring or fit camber compensator, heavy-duty dampers, 4½in or 5½in rim wheels, depending on standard size, heavy-duty anti-roll bar. On Spitfires the Spitfire Mk4 rear spring can be used in conjunction with the stiffer anti-roll bar from the Mk4.
Vitesse/GT6 (wishbone rear)	5½in rim wheels, radial tyres, uprated dampers.
Triumph 1300, 1500 and Toledo	Uprated dampers, radial tyres.
TR range (non-independent)	5½in wide wheels, radial tyres, uprated dampers, front anti-roll bar.
TR range (IRS)	5½in rim wheels, radial tyres, uprated dampers. TR5 and 250 only: front anti-roll bar.
Triumph 2000 and PI	5½in rim wheels, radial tyres, uprated front struts, stiffer rear dampers, front anti-roll bar (not for power-steering models).

Vauxhall: All Vauxhalls listed use coil springs front and rear with independent double-wishbone suspension at the front and a live back axle well located by four links.

Viva HB	Uprated dampers, 5in rim wheels, radial tyres.
Viva 1600 OHC and 2000 GT	Uprated dampers, 5½in rim wheels, radial tyres.
Victor 1600 and 2000 and Ventora	Uprated dampers, 5½in rim wheels, radial tyres.

3
BRAKES

The average modern car has pretty good brakes as standard equipment. They are also versatile: besides being designed to stop the car efficiently from its maximum speed under all normal conditions, they will incorporate pads or linings which will wear well, will not squeal, grab, or cause radio static. The braking will also be so set up that good retardation is available at moderate pedal pressures. If the engine is reworked slightly to improve the car's performance (say, a 10 per cent improvement in acceleration and no more than 5mph on the top speed) the chances are that the standard braking system will be able to cope with it—providing it is in first-class working order.

In Chapter 1, some basic checks were given to establish whether or not the car was pulling up in a straight line. As a starting point, we will take a car with drum brakes all round, and assume that it does not pull up straight. When this happens, it is likely that one of the hydraulic wheel cylinders, which press the shoes against the drums, has sprung a leak. The leaking fluid—which, broadly speaking, is a mixture of vegetable oil and alcohol—will have coated the inside of the drum and some will have been absorbed by the linings. When one brake is lubricated like this and its opposite number on the same axle is maintaining its grip, there is an obvious tendency for the good brake to pull the car round in a circle each time you push the pedal. A further symptom is a steady drop in the level of hydraulic fluid in the reservoir.

Obviously, this condition has to be corrected before any extra power is extracted from the engine. But before you start pulling the braking system to pieces, make one further test on the road to determine whether your lazy brake drum is at the front or rear. Accelerate to 20mph, put the gear lever in neutral and apply the handbrake hard. If the car *still* pulls to one side, the trouble is at the rear, if it does not, the trouble is at the front.

The brake drums on most cars can be taken off easily after removing the road wheel and undoing a couple of brake-drum locating screws. It is sometimes necessary to back off the brake adjuster to give a little extra clearance between the shoes and the drum, after which the drum can be pulled off the wheel studs.

Unfortunately, it is not *always* this simple. Austin/Morris

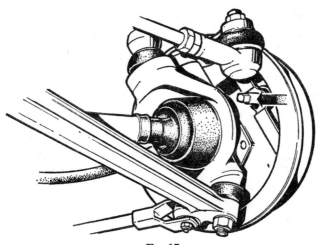

Fig 17

Before removing a brake drum, it may be necessary to back off the adjustment. This is the squared adjuster used on the
Mini

1100s and 1300s, for instance, require a special puller to take off the rear brake drums because the hub is integral with the drum. And on some other cars, self-adjusting brakes are used at the rear, and, depending on the type, may need to be 'de-adjusted' before the drum will come off. In case of difficulty, it is a wise move to make a friend of the storeman at your local dealer, so that at times like this you can study the diagrams in the parts' manual. Better still, if you buy the workshop manual for your car (these are now available for all current British cars) all will be revealed.

Once you have the drum off, a leaking cylinder is easily spotted. To get it out, you will have to remove the brake shoes, and if you are not familiar with brake-shoe layouts this is the

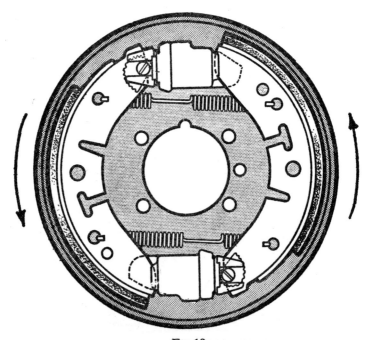

FIG 18

Typical two-leading-shoe drum brake layout. Note the position of the linings on the shoes; they are fitted so that they appear to have 'slipped' in the direction of wheel rotation

stage where you get a notebook and pencil and make a very careful note of how the various components are assembled. Pay particular attention to the position of the linings on the shoes—some are biased and it is possible to assemble the shoes back-to-front—and make a note of which holes the pull-off springs fit into, the method of engagement, and in the event of a spring being asymetrical, note which side the coil goes.

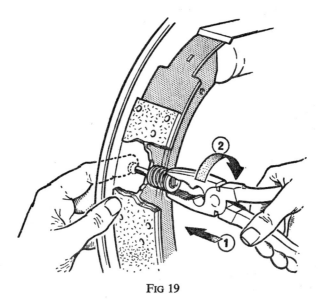

FIG 19

Some shoes are located by steady springs which are detached using pliers. The washer is pushed in (1) and then turned through 90 degrees (2) to release

Depending on the brake, the shoes might be located by steady springs which must be uncoupled with a pair of pliers before the brake shoe is levered off using a large screwdriver. You will now be able to get at the leaking cylinder which may be secured with a spring clip behind the back-plate, or held by a couple of bolts.

The cylinder will still be connected to the flexible hydraulic pipe. To prevent the loss of a lot of fluid and avoid unnecessary

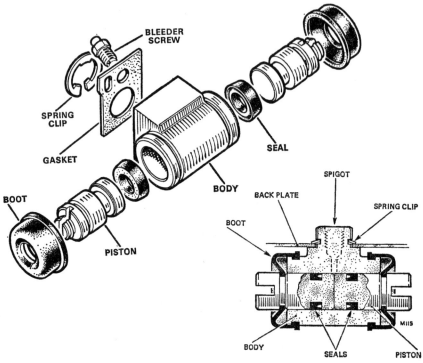

FIG 20

A double-acting hydraulic wheel cylinder looks like this when dismantled. Single-acting cylinders as shown in Fig 18 have only one piston. The spring clip is a tough component and is best levered from its slot (see inset) using a screwdriver. If the clip is corroded, it may break during removal so it is wise to have a few new ones before starting work

air getting into the system, it is best to squeeze up this pipe, and the ideal tool to use for this job is a Girling hose clamp. It is possible to use a self-gripping clamp, such as a Mole wrench, as an alternative. But if you do this, use something fairly soft— such as a couple of strips of timber or hardboard—between the wrench jaws and the pipe, otherwise there is a danger of the sharp jaw edge damaging the pipe.

There are two ways of dealing with a leaking cylinder. Either you can fit a new set of hydraulic rubber seals, which will cost very little, or you can fit a new cylinder. My own preference is to fit a new cylinder, since the new seals will not cure the trouble if there is a tiny scratch in the bore of the existing cylinder. New cylinders for most popular cars cost around £1.50.

Where a cylinder has leaked, you will also have to renew both sets of brake linings on the axle. There are two ways of

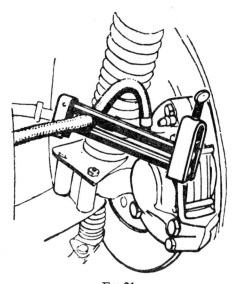

FIG 21

Girling brake shoe clamp in use. It is designed to avoid bruising the flexible brake hose

going about this job, too. It is cheapest to buy a set of brake linings and rivets and fit them yourself to the brake shoes. Alternatively, you can buy, on an exchange basis, a set of shoes with new linings ready fitted. The slightly more expensive ready-lined shoes are preferable, since the linings will have been ground to conform exactly to the shape of the drum and the better fit will give more stopping power. New linings should be used gently for about 200 miles until they have 'bedded in'.

Although leaking fluid is the main cause of brakes pulling, it is not the only possibility. The other main contenders are a seized wheel cylinder or incorrect assembly of the brake shoes. A seized cylinder is easily checked. Lever the brake shoe out of the way, put a screwdriver into the slot that engages with the brake-shoe tip and try to turn the piston in the cylinder. A seized one will not move.

Incorrect assembly of shoes is possible on a number of cars, and was a common reason for the early BMC Minis to pull to one side. On these cars, the lining is not centrally mounted on the shoe, but is biased towards one end, as shown in Fig 18.

If the shoes on one wheel are fitted the wrong way round—and all the necessary mountings are there to allow this to be done—the self-servo action of the linings is altered and the car will pull to one side.

Another cause of pulling (and squealing) drum brakes is lack of shoe-tip lubrication. All modern drum brakes are of the sliding-shoe type, but rust and dirt can prevent the shoes from sliding so that their braking output is affected (and the linings wear tapered); if this happens on only one side the car will pull to the other side. To keep these surfaces clean and assist sliding, a little of an appropriate type of grease, such as that sold in small tubes by Girling, should be applied on assembly.

Brake Bleeding

If the hydraulic system has been broken into by undoing a pipe, some air will have got in and this must be bled out, otherwise the pedal will be spongy in action and in extreme cases may go straight to the floor when you apply the brakes. The copybook method of bleeding the brakes requires a helper, a length of rubber tube, a brake spanner to loosen each bleed screw, some new hydraulic fluid of the correct type and a jam-jar.

On cars with drums all round, begin with the wheel furthest from the master cylinder (the nearside rear on right-hand-drive cars). Attach a tube to the bleed screw and lead the free end

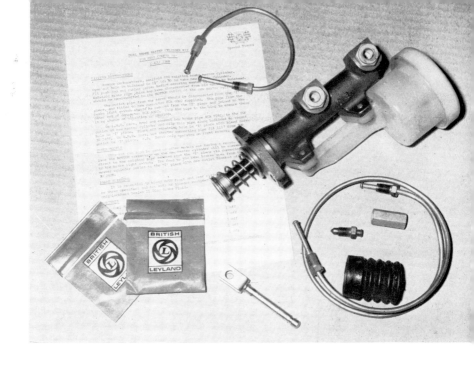

Page 67 (*above*) Mini dual-line braking kit as it comes from British Leyland Special Tuning; (*below*) and as it looks when fitted in place of the normal single-line Mini brake master-cylinder

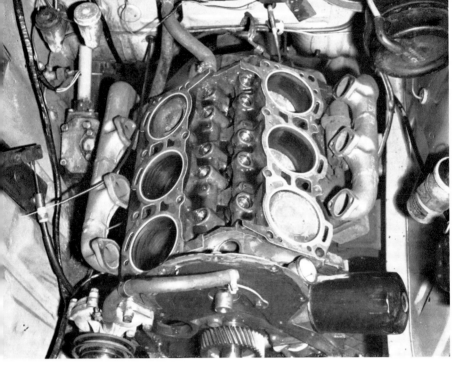

Page 68   (*above*) A three-litre Ford V6 engine fitted into a Cortina Mk1 engine bay. The welded-up exhaust manifolds were from a V4 Corsair engine; (*below*) four hungry mouths. Two twin-choke 40 DCOE Weber carburettors at full throttle on the test bed. The engine is a British Leyland 1275cc unit with a Special Tuning 8 port head

FIG 22

When bleeding brakes, the bleed screw should be tightened when no further bubbles come from the pipe and while the pedal is held down. It is necessary only moderately to tighten the screw, incidentally. Overtightening will strip the threads in the wheel cylinder

into the jam-jar into which you have poured a small quantity of hydraulic fluid. It is important that the end of the tube is immersed in this fluid and it helps if a short length of metal pipe is pushed in the end to act as a weight. Check that the fluid reservoir is topped up, then undo the bleed screw about one turn and get the helper to press the pedal. The way that the pedal is pressed varies with the braking system. Lockheed recommend that the pedal is pressed slowly to the floor and allowed to return after a short pause. Girling, on the other hand, have a different approach. On their CV (centre valve) master cylinder, they suggest you do a sort of 'cha-cha-cha' on the pedal, first pushing it down hard to the floor and following this with three short rapid strokes, after which the foot is slid off the pedal so it can snap back to its stop before you start the process again. The quick action dislodges any air bubbles which may form round the return spring in the master cylinder.

Girling also produce another master cylinder, coded CB. On

E

this one the procedure is to press the pedal slowly to the floor, and allow it to return slowly. There should then be a pause of about three or four seconds, after which the action is repeated. For identification purposes, the CV cylinder is always made from aluminium alloy, whereas the CB is of cast-iron construction.

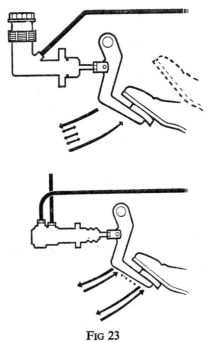

FIG 23

When Girling brakes are being bled, a different pedal action is used, depending on whether the system has a CV master cylinder (*top*) or a CB cylinder

When no further air bubbles come from the end of the tube, tighten the bleed screw while your helper holds the pedal down. Top up the reservoir (the level must never drop below half-full) and repeat the process on the other wheels, finishing with the wheel nearest the master cylinder.

On cars with disc brakes at the front and drums at the rear, the discs are bled first, generally starting with the one nearest the master cylinder. On cars with dual-line braking, the sequence may be different and the handbook should be consulted.

Disc Brakes

A car with disc brakes that pulls to one side is most likely to be suffering from a seized hydraulic piston. The quickest way to check this is to block up the car, remove the road wheel, and, at the disc brake caliper, check the movement of the pistons by inserting a small screwdriver blade between the pad and the disc. It may be necessary to remove some pad-retaining springs to do this. Now see if the pad can be moved away from the

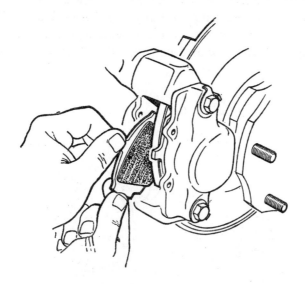

Fig 24

Worn disc pads are generally easier to replace than worn drum-brake linings. On most Lockheed and Girling calipers, pads are withdrawn after removing the locating pins and—on this Lockheed caliper—the pad retaining springs

disc. If you can gently lever it back and retract the piston into its bore about $\frac{1}{16}$in the piston is not seized.

Most disc-brake pads should be renewed when the lining material is worn to within $\frac{1}{8}$in of the backing plate. The exceptions are the Dunlop Series 1 and 2 disc pads which should be renewed when the lining material is $\frac{1}{4}$in thick. The reason for this is that the pistons have limited travel, and if you do not change the pads in time the point is reached at which you cannot apply the brakes.

The fitting of new pads is generally pretty straightforward. On Lockheed and Girling twin-piston calipers it is merely necessary to remove the locking pins and any pad retaining springs and pull the pads out from the calipers, although there are a few exceptions where the complete caliper must be removed. It is wise to clean the pad recesses and check the pistons for leakage which, fortunately, is fairly rare. On Lockheed calipers, where the chrome-plated piston is liable to become corroded, the exposed section should be cleaned with brake fluid before

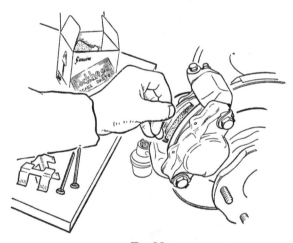

FIG 25

After cleaning the pistons and retracting them, new pads are slipped into place. Where applicable, new split pins and retaining springs are usually supplied in brake pad kits

the pistons are pushed back into the caliper to make way for the new, thicker, pads. The correct tool for this job is a piston retractor, although as an alternative it is possible to use a large screwdriver, providing you take care not to tilt the piston in its bore and jam it.

Pushing the piston back displaces a large volume of hydraulic fluid from the caliper and this can be bled off by loosening the bleed screw at the caliper about half a turn while pressure is being exerted on the piston. Displaced fluid comes out of the bleed screw, which is tightened when the piston has been pushed back sufficiently, and while fluid is still coming out. This procedure will prevent air getting in. The same method is adopted each time you retract a piston.

All that remains now is to fit the new pads with any shims

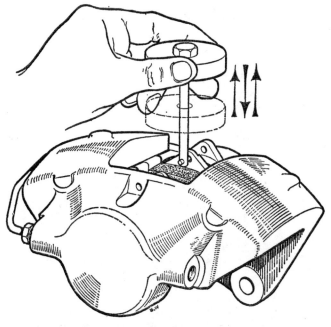

FIG 26

Dunlop disc pads are best removed using this small impact puller, which Girling can supply

that go between the backing plate and the piston, pump the pedal to take up any free play between the pistons and pads, and top up the reservoir.

As always, there are exceptions to the above guide. Dunlop pads sometimes need a special impact-type pad removal tool to get them from the calipers, and Girling, who produce Dunlop disc brakes now, can supply the special tool which has the part number 64932137. It is also important when pushing back Dunlop pistons to avoid damaging the raised spigot in the piston centre, otherwise brake binding may occur. Again, there is a special piston retracting tool, part no 64932392, which will also fit all Girling calipers.

So far, I have dealt with brakes which seem to be in need of attention. If the 20mph sudden-stop test indicates that all is well, it is still worth confirming this by checking under the car that there is no chafing of the flexible hydraulic hoses, that there

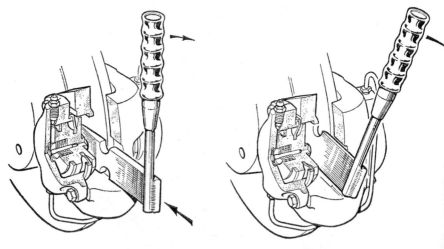

FIG 27

Most disc caliper pistons can be retracted by carefully bearing against them with a large screwdriver blade. But Dunlop pistons have a raised section in the centre which can be easily damaged if this is done. Notches in the Girling piston retracting tool allow the piston to be eased back without any contact with the centre spigot

are no signs of leaks at the unions on the metal pipes, that the pipes are free from corrosion and that all securing nuts and bolts are tight.

The following fault-finder is based on a Girling chart.

Fault	Cause	Cure
Hard pedal—poor braking.	Incorrect linings, glazed linings or linings wet, greasy or not bedded-in, servo unit inoperative, seized caliper pistons, worn dampers allowing wheel bounce.	Replace shoes or if glazed, lightly rub down with rough sandpaper. See chart on page 83 for servo faults. Repair caliper, fit new dampers.
Brake pulling.	Seized pistons, leaking wheel cylinder, vibration in linings, unsuitable tyres or pressures, worn dampers, loose brake mountings, greasy linings, damaged drums, damaged suspension or steering.	Check tyre pressures, renew seized/leaking cylinders, replace contaminated linings, check for excess movement in suspension/steering. Renew damaged drums, fit new dampers.
Fall in fluid level.	Worn disc pads, external leak, leak in servo unit.	Check pads for wear and examine fluid lines and wheel cylinders for leaks. See servo chart.
Uneven or excessive pad wear.	Discs corroded (by salt). Disc badly scored—perhaps after linings have been worn down to the backing plate. Pads require changing.	Check disc for uneven surface, renew if scoring is excessive. Interchange pads to even out wear.
Brake fade.	Incorrect linings. Overloaded vehicle.	Replace shoes, decrease vehicle load. See chart on p 88 for anti-fade linings.
Spongy pedal.	Air in system. Badly lined shoes. Distorted shoes. Faulty drums. Movement at master cylinder mounting.	Bleed air from system, check master cylinder mounting, shoes and drums.
Long pedal travel.	*Disc brakes:* Disc 'run out' pushing pads back. Distorted damping shims. Misplaced dust covers.	Have disc run-out checked by a specialist: it should not exceed ·004in.
	Drum brakes: Brakes need adjustment. Fluid leak. Worn or swollen seals in master cylinder. Blocked vent in reservoir cap. Fluid contaminated.	Check adjustment, filler vent and for fluid leak. Renew seals if necessary and change fluid.

Fault	Cause	Cure
Brakes binding.	Maladjustment. No clearance at master cylinder pushrod. Seals swollen. Seized pistons. Shoe return springs weak or broken. Faulty servo. Sliding wheel cylinders jammed. Gummed-up hand-brake linkage.	Check brake adjustment and handbrake linkage. Examine clearance at master cylinder pushrod, check for seized pistons or weak shoe return springs. See Servo chart. Free off wheel cylinders and hand-brake.

Improvements

When a car has been reworked to go a lot faster than standard something may have to be done to improve its stopping power. As with suspension systems, the amount of work this involves depends on how good the standard item is. Some cars have only small reserves in the braking department, others can put a considerably greater-than-standard load on the brakes with no ill effects. Any problems which arise from over-working a standard braking system can be blamed on the extra build-up of heat generated by applying the brakes harder and from higher speeds.

Adjustment On cars with drum brakes all round, correct adjustment is essential for fast motoring. The reason is that the more the temperature increases, the more the drums expand. And they expand *away* from the shoes, so the clearance increases. During normal everyday motoring the small amount of drum expansion is compensated for by a slight increase in pedal travel, which goes unnoticed. But if the brakes are used hard, drum temperatures may reach 400°C and if at the same time the brakes are in need of adjustment, it is possible for the pedal to come to the end of its travel—usually the toe board—in taking up the clearance between the shoes and the drum.

Admittedly, this sort of situation will not suddenly happen. It is bound to be a progressive process since several hard brake applications will be needed to heat up the drum. So this is some consolation. But in the event of disappointing performance from drum brakes always check the adjustment first.

Fluid Boiling It is possible for drum brakes to be correctly adjusted and still the pedal goes almost to the toe-board when the brakes heat up. In this instance, the trouble is probably due to boiling of the brake fluid. New brake fluid has a boiling point in excess of 260°C and in this state it is unlikely to boil.

The problem arises when the fluid is old, since in ageing it will have absorbed a quantity of water which lowers its boiling point. When hard-working brakes boil this fluid, vapour forms as bubbles in the hydraulic system and when an attempt is made to apply the brakes these bubbles must be compressed before the system will work. If the bubbles are small, all the driver will notice is a slightly spongy feel to the pedal and an increase in travel. But if there is a lot of vapour in the system, the driver will find his foot on the toe-board and no brakes. If this happens, it may be possible to get back some braking by pumping the pedal quickly. One interesting side-effect of boiling fluid is that once the brakes have cooled, the vapour condenses and no evidence remains.

Brake fluid is changed by opening a bleed screw and pumping it out with the pedal. When the reservoir is nearly empty it should be topped up with new fluid. Pump until all the dirty fluid has been expelled and new fluid comes through un-clouded before topping up again and bleeding the brakes.

Fade If the brakes are correctly adjusted and the system is full of new fluid yet you feel the stopping power at high speeds still needs improvement, the car is probably suffering from brake fade. Fade is caused by over-heating of the linings or pads. It is more likely to occur on cars with drum brakes all round, since drums do not dissipate their heat so quickly as discs.

When linings or pads become excessively hot, chemical changes take place at the surface which have an effect on the friction which the driver relies upon for his stopping power.

Usually the resin in the lining is the first constituent to be affected by the heat. Given some time to cool and some moderate usage to wear away the damaged surface, the linings may recover their normal friction. But if the fade was severe, the friction material may have been permanently damaged and need renewal.

On standard production cars with standard engines, brake fade is not common. The average modern brake lining is normally suitable for use at continuous temperatures up to 175°C and maximum temperatures for short periods up to 400°C. In practice, the average motorist seldom gets the temperature of the brake drums much above 175°C. But on a rally car or a modified road car, brake fade is more of a possibility and the answer is to fit anti-fade competition-type linings or pads. Anti-fade linings do what they say—they extend the point at which fade takes place—but because they are designed primarily to operate at high temperatures, when compared with 'softer' road-going linings they do not have so many fringe benefits.

The first time you drive a car with anti-fade linings you may be disappointed. For they do not feel particularly good at moderate speeds. In fact, they nearly always need greater pedal pressures to bring the car to a stop than the standard material. Happily, the heavy pedal problem is easily cured by fitting a brake servo which is detailed later on. Strangely, serious competition drivers rarely use servos; they prefer a heavy, direct-acting pedal because they say it gives a better 'feel' of the road-surface.

The other main characteristic of anti-fade linings is that they need to be continuously worked hard for maximum efficiency. The one exception is when bedding-in new linings, which should be used gently for a period to prevent local hot-spots forming on the new surface of the material. Once the material has bedded over 95 per cent of the surface, the next stage on drum brakes is to remove the drums and blow out any brake dust—this obviously is not necessary on discs—after which the brakes are used hard to condition the lining surface until the friction stabilises and smooth, even braking is obtained. From this point on, the brakes should always be used pretty firmly, otherwise the conditioned surface of the lining will wear away and friction will become variable.

There are some 'in-between' linings and disc pads which are not so critical in use, and I have included a list of high-performance pad and lining recommendations for a number of popular cars at the end of this chapter. The list refers to Ferodo materials which, although they are not the only anti-fade materials available, are the most widely used and have been almost universal wear for Grand Prix cars for many years. The DS 11 pad was developed for Formula 1 cars and is now available for a number of road cars for rally use. The drum brake equivalent is the VG95/1 which was widely used for the brakes of racing cars before the days of disc brakes, and was initially developed for the land-speed record cars of the mid-1930s.

Brake Boosters On its own, a brake booster or servo will not increase the efficiency of the brakes. Its function is purely to lighten the load needed at the pedal and make the brakes easier to apply, and it is particularly worthwhile if anti-fade linings or pads are fitted.

Both Lockheed and Girling make boosters which tap their power from the engine inlet manifold and are plumbed into the hydraulic pipes between the master cylinder and the four-way junction where the pipe-work splits to feed the front and rear wheels. On cars with dual braking systems, the layout may be different and the brake manufacturers should be consulted.

The most common servo ratio used on road-going cars is $1\frac{1}{2}$:1. This gives the same retardation with, say, 50lb pedal pressure as a non-boosted system would with 75lb pressure at the pedal. Other ratios are available if more servo assistance is needed, although before ordering one it is worth having a word with the technical service department of the appropriate brake manufacturer to see what they recommend. Incidentally, if you

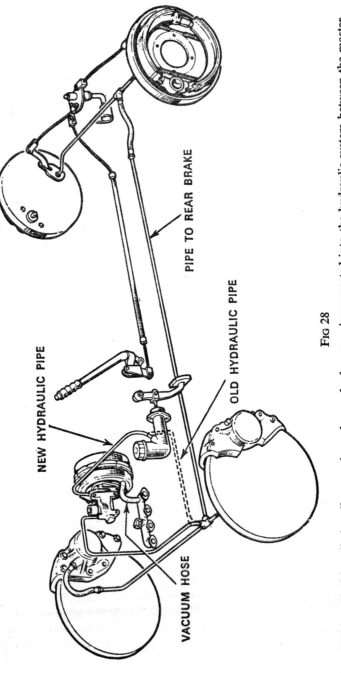

PIPE TO REAR BRAKE

NEW HYDRAULIC PIPE

OLD HYDRAULIC PIPE

VACUUM HOSE

Fig 28

This typical installation diagram shows how a brake servo is connected into the hydraulic system between the master cylinder and the four-way connection which feeds fluid to the front and rear brakes

have special preferences, it is possible to fit a Girling servo to a Lockheed braking system and vice-versa. When this is done, the brake fluid already in use in the system is retained.

Fitting a servo yourself is not difficult and although the brake manufacturers will generally encourage you to have one fitted by one of their agents, they do include fitting instructions with each kit of parts.

If you are doing the job at home, there are three principal stages to the work. First, the servo unit must be positioned on the car. Servos are fairly bulky and this is not quite so simple as it seems. On some cars, for instance—the Mini is one—there is so little space to spare under the bonnet that the unit must be fitted above the offside front wheel in the wheel arch. The exposed position means that the servo has to be enclosed in a plastic bag and the air filter extended under the bonnet. Again, consult the technical service department of Lockheed or Girling if you have difficulty finding a suitable position for the unit.

The next step is to make the vacuum connection to the inlet manifold. Most major manufacturers put a spare plug into the inlet so that it can be unscrewed and replaced by a suitable adaptor if a servo is fitted. Depending on the car, the adaptor may be supplied either by the servo manufacturer or the car maker.

If there is no plug, you will have to do the job the hard way. This involves taking off the inlet manifold, drilling it and tapping it to accept the threaded take-off pipe. The pipe should be fixed so that the flexible hose that connects it to the servo curves up from the manifold before dropping down to the servo. This prevents it picking up and holding any neat petrol. Clean any swarf or metal particles from the manifold before refitting it.

Up to now we have not broken into the hydraulic system, and if you want to leave off at this stage the car can be driven if the take-off pipe in the manifold has been temporarily closed. The simplest way to do this is to push a short length of hose over the pipe, blocking the other end of the hose with a suitable bolt.

The third stage is to connect up the hydraulic pipes and bleed the air from the system. Two lengths of steel hydraulic pipe, complete with unions and any necessary adaptors will be included in the kit and, depending on where you have sited the servo, these may be of about the right length or much too long. Pipes that are over-long must be shortened by a braking specialist, who will have the equipment needed to reflare the end of the pipe at the union so that it will make an air-tight joint. It is definitely not wise to attempt to reflare a pipe yourself with a centre-punch, since this cannot bell out the pipe sufficiently without cracking it. Similarly, the use of a solderless olive on a brake pipe (these are sometimes used on fuel lines) is highly dangerous, since this type of joint cannot withstand the pressures in a hydraulic system.

If the brake pipes are only a little longer than you need, they may be horizontally coiled to take up the surplus length, and a

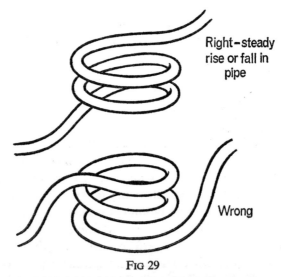

FIG 29

The right and wrong way to coil a hydraulic pipe.
Where hydraulic pipes are coiled to take up excess length,
the coil should be wound so that there is a steady rise or
fall of fluid. This prevents air bubbles collecting at high-
points

tidy job can be made of this if the pipe is coiled round a former, such as an old aerosol tin. The diameter of the coil should be at least two inches, and the direction of the coils should be such that there is a continuous rise or fall of the pipe. With the connections made, all the air must be evacuated from the pipes and servo. It saves a lot of hydraulic fluid if the servo outlet pipe is detached at the four-way connection and the pedal pumped until fluid comes out the pipe. Then, with the pedal held down, the pipe can be re-connected. Next the brakes are bled as described earlier. All brake bleeding should be carried out without the engine running.

Servo Fault Finding

Fault	*Cause*	*Cure*
Hard pedal— apparent lack of assistance with engine running.	Lack of vacuum. Restricted hose. Blocked air inlet. Faulty output piston. Major fault in unit.	Check vacuum connections. Check hose and replace if necessary— fit parts from service kit—examine filter and air inlet—fit new unit.
Slow action of servo unit.	Blocked filter or restricted air inlet. Faulty vacuum hose or connections.	Change filter. Tighten vacuum connections. Replace hose.
Lack of assistance on heavy braking. Servo operating only when engine is running. Poor slow running of engine.	Air leak in servo causing low vacuum. Air leaks in gaskets, non-return valve grommet, rubber sleeve, diaphragm or air valve. Leaking vacuum hoses or faulty non-return valve.	Check for vacuum leaks, if unsuccessful, dismantle and replace all parts in service kit. Tighten vacuum connections. Replace vacuum hose or replace non-return valve.
Loss of fluid.	Failure of a seal or seals in unit or scored bores.	Replace unit or fit a service kit of seals and gaskets.
Pedal pushes back.	Hydraulic inlet and outlet pipe wrongly connected, or fault in unit.	Re-connect pipes or dismantle unit.

After the brakes have been bled you will notice that the pedal has a softer feel to it. This is because of the movement of a valve in the servo and is quite normal. Press the pedal hard with the engine running, and check all joints for leaks before road-testing the vehicle.

Pedal load (lb)	Stopping distance (ft)	
	boosted	unboosted
10	377	377
20	131	178
30	73	104
40	49	80
50	37	58
60	31·7	45
70	*30·2	35
80	31·4	31·7
90	31·4	*30·2
100	30·8	30·2

* = 100 per cent G

FIG 30

These figures show the way a brake booster or servo cuts down a car's stopping distance for the same pedal effort. The servo does not improve brake efficiency, as shown by the car's ability to stop in 30·2ft from 30mph —equivalent to 100 per cent G on a brake meter—with and without a booster fitted. But whereas an un-boosted system needed a 90lb push on the pedal for maximum stopping power, with a booster in the line, the effect was reduced to 70lb. It is interesting that brake efficiency falls off when higher-than-necessary pedal pressures are used with the boosted system. This is due to wheel locking

Dual-line Systems Some classes of motor sport require the competing vehicles to have two independent hydraulic systems so that in the event of failure, say, of a brake pipe leading to a rear wheel, braking would still be available on the front ones. For the road, dual braking can only be regarded as an insurance against sudden brake failure, since it does not improve the standard of braking.

It is only fairly recently that dual-line braking systems began to appear on British cars as standard equipment, although cars exported to North America have been fitted with dual systems for some time to conform with US regulations. This means that the components to convert most British cars are available—

providing the pipe-work is suitably altered to fit a right-hand-drive car, and providing you can get someone to supply them. For it is an unfortunate fact that brake manufacturers do not encourage the average motorist to attempt to improve his braking system, and turn a remarkably deaf ear to requests for parts. Some cars are catered for officially, however. The Lockheed dual-line system available for the Cooper 'S' and other Minis is an example, and is available from British Leyland Special Tuning as a kit. The heart of this conversion is the new master cylinder with separate outlet pipes for the front and rear wheels. The way in which the new master cylinder is plumbed-in depends on whether the car has a brake servo. If it has, the servo cannot supply independent assistance to both circuits, and it is usual to re-route the pipe-work so that it operates only on the front. When this is done on the Mini, the servo works very nearly as well as it did on all four wheels, since most of the braking effort is on the front wheels anyway, and the car has a pressure-limiting valve in the rear pipe-lines to discourage rear-wheel locking.

There is another peculiarity with front/rear dual-line systems. When bleeding the brakes, the front and rear wheel cylinders must be bled at the same time. So if you use the traditional method of brake bleeding already outlined, you will need three operators and two sets of bleeder equipment to do the job.

Short Cuts Once a braking system has been equipped with properly bedded brake linings or pads and all adjustments have been made, you should have a car with a firm, no-nonsense pedal which gives a responsive 'feel' of the road surface when stopping from high speeds. On systems with servo assistance, a slightly softer pedal is allowable, but if the pedal feels spongy or has excessive travel, something is wrong. Fortunately, there is a quick way to find out where the trouble is if you have three Girling hose clamps, or something similar.

One clamp is positioned on each length of flexible hose (on cars with four flexible hoses you will need four clamps). Clamp

F

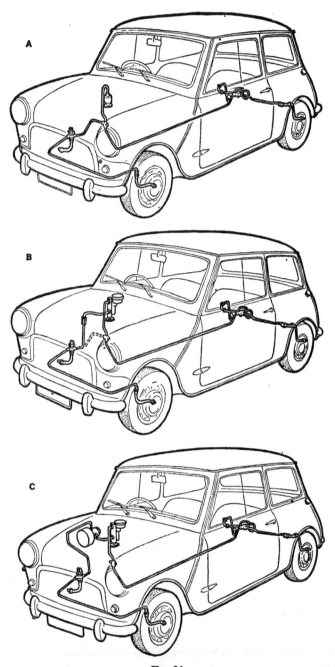

FIG 31

When the Lockheed dual-line braking conversion is carried out on a Mini, the layout is varied if a servo is fitted. Diagram (A) shows the standard layout used on a non-servo Mini, and (B) shows it converted to dual-line operation using the Lockheed master cylinder. In (C) the servo has been re-routed so that it only operates on the front wheels of the dual-line set up

each hose in turn and check the pedal each time. When the sponginess disappears, the last hose you clamped up was the one leading to the trouble-spot. If, with all hoses blocked off by the clamps, the pedal is still spongy, the trouble is in the master cylinder.

The most likely cause of a spongy pedal is air in the system. Where this appears to be confined to one wheel and there are no obvious signs of leakage, it is probable that the wheel cylinder is allowing the air in. One would expect a cylinder that lets air in to allow some fluid to leak out. But, unfortunately, this is not always so, although it will leak fluid eventually, of course. The cure for a suspect cylinder is a new one.

Brake bleeding is normally regarded as at least a two-man job, but it need not be. The easiest way to bleed the brakes on

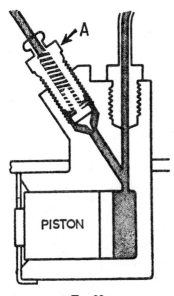

FIG 32

Anatomy of an automatic bleed valve. After loosening
the screw 'A', fluid can be pumped from the system, but
the spring and conical non-return valve prevent air from
entering

your own is to replace the standard bleed screws with automatic bleed valves. These contain a spring-loaded non-return valve which, once the screw is loosened, allows fluid to be pumped out by the brake pedal, but will not allow any air in. They are particularly useful for bleeding air from dual braking systems. In fact, with these valves it is possible to bleed all wheels simultaneously.

Anti-Fade Materials

This table gives recommended Ferodo heavy-duty linings and pads for rally and racing use. For fast road use, rally linings should be fitted if a change is necessary.

| Make and model | Year | Front or rear | Special recommendations | | | |
| | | | Boosted | | Unboosted | |
			Rally	Racing	Rally	Racing
BMC						
Mini & MkII & Clubman	Oct 1964/71	F	VG95/1	VG95/1	AM4	AM4
Elf & Hornet	March 1963/9	R	VG95/1	VG95/1	AM8	AM8
Mini	1959/64	F	VG95/1	VG95/1	AM4	AM4
Elf & Hornet	1962/March 1963	R	VG95/1	VG95/1	AM8	AM8
Mini Cooper 'S' and	1963/71	F	DS11	DS11	DS11	2426F
1275 GT		R	VG95/1	VG95/1	VG95/1	VG95/1
Mini Cooper	March 1963/70	F	DS11	DS11	DS11	DS11
		R	VG95/1	VG95/1	VG95/1	VG95/1
Mini Cooper	1962/March 1963	F	DS11	DS11	DS11	DS11
		R	VG95/1	VG95/1	VG95/1	VG95/A
A40 Series II	1962/7	F	VG95/1	VG95/1	AM4	AM4
		R	VG95/1	VG95/1	AM8	AM8
1100	1962/8	F	DS11	DS11	DS11	2426F
		R	VG95/1	VG95/1	VG95/1	VG95/1
1100 MkII	1968/71	F	DS11	DS11	DS11	DS11
1300 & GT	1968/71	R	VG95/1	VG95/1	VG95/1	VG95/1
Maxi 1500 & 1750	1969/71	F	DS11	DS11	DS11	DS11
		R	VG95/1	VG95/1	VG95/1	VG95/1
1800 & MkII	1964/71	F	DS11	DS11	DS11	DS11
		R	VG95/1	VG95/1	VG95/1	VG95/1
1800S	1969/71	F	DS11	DS11	DS11	DS11
		R	VG95/1	VG95/1	VG95/1	VG95/1
Sprite MkII, III & IV	1963/71	F	DS11	DS11	DS11	2426F
Midget & MkII & III	1963/71	R	VG95/1	VG95/1	VG95/1	VG95/1

Make and model	Year	Front or rear	Special recommendations Boosted Rally	Racing	Unboosted Rally	Racing
Sprite MkII & Midget Sprite (948cc)	1961/2 1958/61	F R	VG95/1 VG95/1	VG95/1 VG95/1	AM4 AM8	AM4 AM8
MGB, GT & MkII	1962/71	F R	DS11 VG95/1	DS11 VG95/1	DS11 VG95/1	DS11 VG95/1
MGC	1968/9	F R	DS11 VG95/1	DS11 VG95/1	DS11 VG95/1	DS11 VG95/1
FORD						
Anglia 105E	1959/68	F R	VG95/1 VG95/1	VG95/1 VG95/1	VG95/1 AM4 Each Shoe	VG95/1 AM4 Each Shoe
Super Anglia (1200cc)	1962/8	F	VG95/1	VG95/1	VG95/1	VG95/1
Consul Cortina (1200cc)	1962/4	R	VG95/1	VG95/1	VG95/1	VG95/1
Super Cortina (1500cc)	1963/4	F R	VG95/1 VG95/1	VG95/1 VG95/1	VG95/1 VG95/1	VG95/1 VG95/1
Cortina (1200cc)	Jan to June 1965	F	DS11	DS11	2430F	2430F
Super Cortina (1500cc)	Jan to June 1965	R	VG95/1	VG95/1	VG95/1	VG95/1
Cortina (1200cc)	July 1965/6	F	DS11	DS11	DS11	2430F
Super Cortina (1500cc)	July 1965/6	R	VG95/1	VG95/1	VG95/1	VG95/1
Cortina 1300, 1500 & 1600 Capri 1300	1967/70 1969/70	F R	DS11 VG95/1	DS11 VG95/1	DS11 VG95/1	2430F VG95/1
Cortina GT Cortina 1600E Lotus Cortina Corsair V4, GT & 2000E Capri 1300GT, 1600, 1600GT & 2000GT Escort Twin Cam	1966/70 1968/70 1966/70 1966/70 1969/70 1968/70	F R	DS11 VG95/1	DS11 VG95/1	DS11 VG95/1	DS11 VG95/1
Lotus Cortina	1963/5	F R	DS11 VG95/1	DS11 VG95/1	DS11 VG95/1	DS11 VG95/1
Cortina GT Capri, Capri GT Corsair, Corsair GT Classic	1963/5 1963/4 1964/5 1961/3	F R	DS11 VG95/1	DS11 VG95/1	2430F VG95/1	2430F VG95/1
Escort 1100 & 1100 Super	1968/71	F R	VG95/1 VG95/1	VG95/1 VG95/1	VG95/1 VG95/1	VG95/1 VG95/1
Escort 1300 Super	1968/71	F R	VG95/1 VG95/1	VG95/1 VG95/1	VG95/1 VG95/1	VG95/1 VG95/1
Escort 1300 GT	1968/71	F	DS11	DS11	DS11	DS11
Escort (optional disc brakes)	1968/71	R	VG95/1	VG95/1	VG95/1	VG95/1
Cortina 1300, 1600, 1600GT & 2000	1971-	F R	DS11 VG95/1	DS11 VG95/1	DS11 VG95/1	DS11 VG95/1

Make and model	Year	Front or rear	Special recommendations			
			Boosted		Unboosted	
			Rally	Racing	Rally	Racing
ROOTES						
Imp and all variations	1963/71	F	VG95/1	VG95/1	VG95/1	VG95/1
		R	VG95/1	VG95/1	VG95/1	VG95/1
Rapier, Hunter, Minx GT Gazelle, Vogue & Sceptre	1968/71	F	DS11	DS11	DS11	DS11
		R	VG95/1	VG95/1	VG95/1	VG95/1
Rapier III, IIIA, IV & V	Late 1959/67	F	DS11	DS11	DS11	DS11
		R	VG95/1	VG95/1	VG95/1	VG95/1
Alpine V	1966/8	F	DS11	DS11	DS11	DS11
		R	VG95/1	VG95/1	VG95/1	VG95/1
Alpine III & IV	Dec 1963/6	F	DS11	DS11	DS11	DS11
Tiger	1965/7	R	VG95/1	VG95/1	VG95/1	VG95/1
Alpine I & II	1959/63	F	DS11	DS11	DS11	DS11
		R	VG95/1	VG95/1	VG95/1	VG95/1
Avenger & GT	1970–	F	DS11	DS11	DS11	DS11
		R	VG95/1	VG95/1	VG95/1	VG95/1
TRIUMPH						
Herald 1200	1961/70	F	VG95/1	VG95/1	VG95/1	VG95/1
Herald	1959/61	R	VG95/1	VG95/1	VG95/1	VG95/1
Herald 'S'	1961/2					
Herald 12/50	1963/7					
Herald (optional disc brakes)	1961/7	F	DS11	DS11	DS11	DS11
Spitfire 4 & MkII	1962/6	R	VG95/1	VG95/1	VG95/1	VG95/1
Herald 13/60	1968/71	F	DS11	DS11	DS11	DS11
Spitfire MkIII	1967/71	R	VG95/1	VG95/1	VG95/1	VG95/1
1300 & 1300TC	1966/70	F	DS11	DS11	DS11	DS11
		R	VG95/1	VG95/1	VG95/1	VG95/1
Vitesse	1962/6	F	DS11	DS11	DS11	DS11
		R	VG95/1	VG95/1	VG95/1	VG95/1
Vitesse 2 litre & MkII	1967/71	F	DS11	DS11	DS11	DS11
GT6 & MkII	1967/71	R	VG95/1	VG95/1	VG95/1	VG95/1
2000	1964/9	F	DS11	DS11	DS11	DS11
		R	VG95/1	VG95/1	VG95/1	VG95/1
2·5PI Saloon	1969	F	DS11	DS11	DS11	DS11
		R	VG95/1	VG95/1	VG95/1	VG95/1
TR4, TR4A, TR5 & TR6	1962/71	F	DS11	DS11	DS11	DS11
		R	VG95/1	VG95/1	VG95/1	VG95/1
Toledo	1970–	F	VG95/1	VG95/1	VG95/1	VG95/1
		R	VG95/1	VG95/1	VG95/1	VG95/1
1500	1970–	F	DS11	DS11	DS11	DS11
		R	VG95/1	VG95/1	VG95/1	VG95/1
VAUXHALL						
Viva & Viva SL (HA, HB & HC Series)	1964/71	F	VG95/1	VG95/1	AM4	AM4
		R	VG95/1	VG95/1	AM4	AM4
Viva (op disc brakes) Viva 90 & 90SL (HA Series)	1964/6	F	DS11	DS11	DS11	DS11
	1966	R	VG95/1	VG95/1	VG95/1	VG95/1

Make and model	Year	Front or rear	Special recommendations			
			Boosted		Unboosted	
			Rally	Racing	Rally	Racing
Viva (op disc brakes)	1967/71					
Viva 90 & 90SL		F	DS11	DS11	DS11	DS11
(HB Series)	1967/71	R	VG95/1	VG95/1	VG95/1	VG95/1
Viva 1600	1968/71					
Viva GT	1968/70	F	DS11	DS11	DS11	DS11
Victor (FD Series)	1968/71	R	VG95/1	VG95/1	VG95/1	VG95/1
Ventora	1968/71	F	DS11	DS11	DS11	DS11
		R	VG95/1	VG95/1	VG95/1	VG95/1
Victor 101 (FC Series)	1964/7	F	VG95/1	VG95/1	VG95/1	VG95/1
		R	VG95/1	VG95/1	VG95/1	VG95/1
Victor 101 (op disc	Oct 1964/7	F	DS11	DS11	DS11	DS11
brakes) & VX 4/90		R	VG95/1	VG95/1	VG95/1	VG95/1

4

A LITTLE FASTER

It is not difficult to make a car go a little faster. Depending on the engine design, all that is normally required is to make it 'breathe' a little more efficiently. The way in which this is done depends upon the engine, and before we get too bogged down with detail, let us first look at a little basic theory.

The cycles of a four-stroke engine can be crudely labelled suck, squeeze, bang and blow—referred to in more formal language as intake, compression, power and exhaust strokes. The secret of getting extra power from an engine is to create a bigger bang above the piston. This will exert more force on the crankshaft which, in turn, will give more power at the back wheels. There are various ways of doing this. Up to a point, a bigger or more efficient carburettor pushing more mixture down the inlet ports will get a weightier charge of petrol/air mixture into the combustion chamber and provide a bigger bang.

But there are limitations to the effect of big carburettors alone and one of these is the size and lift of the inlet valve. Small valves with a small lift can only let in a certain amount of mixture. If you want to get still more in, the valve must either be

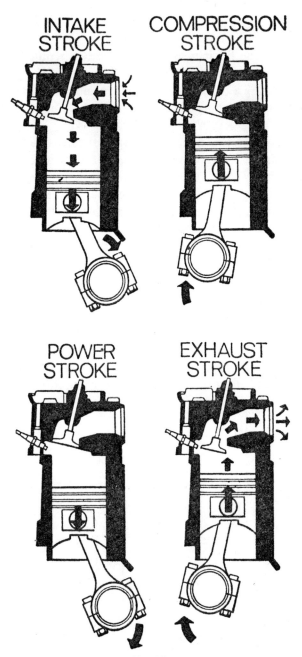

INTAKE STROKE

COMPRESSION STROKE

POWER STROKE

EXHAUST STROKE

Fig 33

The basic action of a four-stroke engine. For small increases in power, the efficiency of the intake and compression strokes is improved

enlarged or the lift increased. Larger valves require modifications to the combustion chamber, while extra lift can be provided by fitting a higher-lift camshaft. A modified camshaft can also alter the duration of valve opening, holding it open for a longer period.

Often there are snags to increasing inlet valve size and lift for a road-going car. Big valves and high-lift camshafts work best at high engine speeds. At slower speeds there is usually a loss of power. On a road-going car with big valves and a high-lift camshaft you may, for instance, have little power below 3,000rpm—corresponding to about 50mph in top gear—and in addition the tick-over would have to be speeded-up considerably to avoid lumpiness.

So most engine tuners reserve big valves and high-lift camshafts for the more advanced stages of road tuning and for competition engines and tackle the problem of getting a bigger bang on the power strokes from a different angle. What they do is reduce the space available above the piston for the mixture to burn in. The process is known as raising the compression ratio, and the effect of squeezing the existing mixture charge a

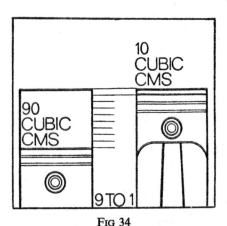

FIG 34

Compression ratio is a comparison of the volume above the piston at BDC (*left*) with the volume above it at TDC

little more is the same as letting more mixture in—you get a bigger push on the piston when it burns.

As can be seen from the diagram (Fig 34) the compression ratio of an engine is simply a way of comparing the volume of air in the cylinder when the piston is at bottom dead centre (BDC) with compressed volume of air when the piston is at TDC.

When virtually all engines had their combustion chambers in the cylinder head, it was comparatively easy to raise the compression ratio. All you did was skim metal from the cylinder head face to reduce the volume of the combustion chamber. But with increased popularity of bowl-in-piston engines, currently fitted to a number of British Ford cars, the combustion chamber is in the piston crown and the cylinder head may be completely flat. In engines such as these, raising the compression ratio becomes a matter of changing pistons or machining the block, which is a major dismantling job and, not, in my view, justified for mild road-going improvements.

On engines where it is difficult to raise the compression ratio, the engine tuners do a 'port and polish' job on the head. This adds up to smoothing out all the casting roughness on the inlet and exhaust ports, and on the inlet side, re-shaping the ports where this is possible to allow greater gas flow at full throttle.

The ideal shape of an inlet port varies with the type of engine. It is generally conceded that the ideal inlet tract should not have any sharp bends in it to slow down the flow, yet at the valve end it should impart a swirl to the mixture as it goes into the combustion chamber, since this turbulence will help the burning of the mixture.

Since a mixture of petrol and air is not a very stable commodity—the mixture strength can vary owing to a number of factors—the ideal inlet port modification is often only arrived at after a period of trial-and-error. The professionals generally use a flow rig and measure the airflow through the port during various stages of modification until the maximum flow is obtained.

You can use the kitchen sink for this job—Bill Blydenstein, who now specialises in tuning Vauxhall cars, once flow-matched the ports on a Borgward engine by pouring a measured quantity of water through each one and noting the time taken for the water to get through. The car was startlingly successful on the race circuit.

Another method of using a flow rig is to introduce an aerosol spray of black or white paint into the air-stream. This means that besides measuring the rate of flow, you can also get an idea of where the air is going on its way through the port, since any section picking up more than its fair share of paint is causing an obstruction. This method is used by Speedwell & Piper.

Valve Springs Most production engines cannot be revved much above the speed where they produce their maximum power because of a condition known as valve float. What happens is that the valve spring is not strong enough at this engine speed fully to close the valve before the camshaft does another revolution and opens it again. The result is that compression is lost and the power of the engine drops. It is a useful safety valve in that it prevents production engines from being damaged by heavy-footed drivers.

If heavier valve springs than standard are fitted the engine's useful rev-range is extended. On their own, these will not give any more power, but they will allow the car to be accelerated to higher speeds in the intermediate gears, and this can improve the acceleration.

Let us assume, for instance, that valve float sets in at 40mph in second gear. So, for maximum acceleration, you go to 40mph in second, then change into third, which drops the engine revs down to, say, 3,300. Now look at the same situation with stronger valve springs which allow 44mph to be reached in second. A change-up at this point means you hit third gear at about 3,700rpm. The engine will be producing more power at this speed than at 3,300rpm, so you will get a slight gain in acceleration. It must not be forgotten that even if it is past peak power, the average engine will still accelerate from 40–44mph in second quicker than it can in third gear.

Exhaust Systems So far most of the emphasis has been on improving the inlet side, and little has been said about the exhaust. This is because the inlet charge has got only atmospheric pressure, or, if you like, the suction of the descending piston to draw it into the combustion chamber. The exhaust, on the other hand, which is a by-product of the power stroke that has already generated sufficient energy to ram the piston to the bottom of its stroke, does not normally need much help on its way out. And for this reason, exhaust valves are normally smaller than inlet valves.

Bearing this in mind, it may seem surprising that most performance cars use high-efficiency exhaust manifolds, where possible, with an individual exhaust pipe for each cylinder. The reason is not immediately obvious until you know about valve overlap. There is an instant when the piston is near the top of its exhaust stroke at which both inlet and exhaust valves are open at the same time. What happens is that the inlet valve begins to open before the exhaust has completely closed.

The thinking behind this is that the residue of exhaust on its way out will help draw in some of the fresh petrol/air mixture through the inlet. This is where a high-efficiency exhaust system comes in. Because it allows the exhaust gas to get away quicker than it can in the one-piece cast-iron manifold fitted to most saloons, it gives more pull to the inlet charge during the overlap. This, in turn, means better filling of the combustion chamber and more power.

If you are contemplating building a racing engine, there is much more that can be done with exhaust manifolds. For instance, by tuning the lengths of the pipes it is possible to get the negative (or vacuum) pulse that follows the discharge of exhaust gas into the pipe to further help draw in the inlet charge during the valve overlap. For production cars, tuning of this sort is not usually possible as there is rarely room for the ideal

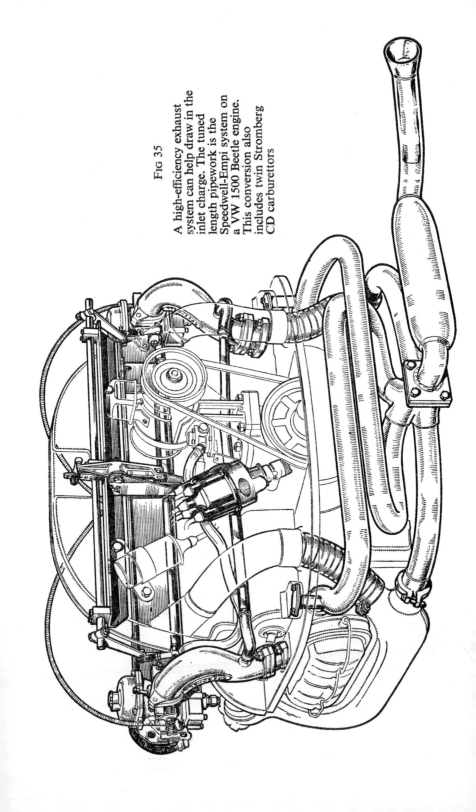

FIG 35

A high-efficiency exhaust system can help draw in the inlet charge. The tuned length pipework is the Speedwell-Empi system on a VW 1500 Beetle engine. This conversion also includes twin Stromberg CD carburettors

pipe lengths. It is possible, however, to improve matters in another way on a road car. For where a restrictive baffle-type silencer is fitted, replacing it by a straight-through silencer will improve the gas flow and is likely to raise the power output slightly. As its name suggests, a straight-through silencer allows the exhaust gas an almost uninterrupted flow, but at the same time absorbs much of the exhaust noise. This is done by perforating the exhaust pipe where it goes through the silencer box, and packing the surrounding area with sound-absorbent material. For best results, the tail-pipe diameter of a straight-through silencer should be the same as the entry pipe.

Summing-up so far, for a small power increase the options are to work on the cylinder head, improve the carburation and maybe fit a high-efficiency exhaust system. Depending on which tuning shop you patronise, you will be encouraged either to sort out the cylinder head first, or make some alterations to the existing carburettor, or perhaps bolt on a bigger one. Since working on the carburettor involves the least dismantling, we will deal with this first.

Carburettors

Possibly two of the most popular carburettors for fitting to road-going modified engines are the SU and the Stromberg CD. Both are constant-vacuum units and use a tapered needle operating in one jet to meter the fuel supply.

The principle of operation is simple. The needle is raised and lowered by the depression—or vacuum—in the inlet manifold. In the case of the SU, this is caused to operate on the upper surface of a large-diameter piston. The tapered needle is attached to the underside of the piston assembly and the effect of this arrangement is that the more the throttle is opened, the higher the piston is raised by manifold depression, so providing a richer mixture. Closing the throttle reduces the depression acting on the piston, so that the needle is lowered into the jet by the combined action of the weight of the piston and a return spring. The result of this is to reduce the supply of fuel.

At the same time, the shaping of the piston assembly is such that the lower section varies the cross-section of the choke tube, allowing a large volume of air into the carburettor with the throttle open, and a correspondingly smaller volume as the throttle is closed. The diagram shows the principle.

The Stromberg CD works in the same way, but instead of a piston it uses a flexible plastic diaphragm to raise and lower the needle. Both carburettors have a damper to slow down the initial

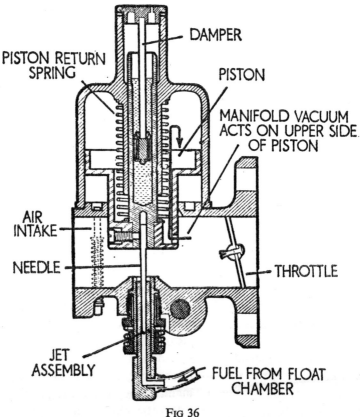

Fig 36
Cross-section of an HS type SU carburettor

lift of the piston. This allows the depression to draw a richer shot of fuel from the jet and this acts in the same way as an accelerator pump, giving a rich mixture for acceleration. The big advantage of this type of carburettor is that, by altering the taper of the needle, the mixture strength can be varied throughout all engine speed ranges. Unfortunately, needle dimensions are extremely critical, the taper being quoted to the nearest 10,000th of an inch at $\frac{1}{8}$in intervals along its length, so that modifying the taper is not the sort of job you can do using an electric drill and a strip of emery cloth.

In fact, what normally happens is that engine tuners settle for a needle from the range that SU or Stromberg have to offer. In this context, SU, which has been building this type of carburettor the longest, has nearly 450 needles to choose from, whereas Stromberg at the time of writing was offering around 220. For obvious trade reasons, SU and Stromberg CD needles are not interchangeable. A list of suggested needles for a variety of engines is given in Chapter 7.

One of the most popular cars for carburettor-swapping is the British Leyland Mini, and controlled tests have shown that a big carburettor on the 848cc engine can give a useful uplift in performance. In fact, even fitting another needle to the existing 1$\frac{1}{4}$in SU carburettor has an effect, as shown by this series of tests carried out by *Practical Motorist* magazine.

First, performance figures were taken using the stock HS2 SU carburettor fitted with the standard EB needle and red spring. Then the British Leyland-recommended rich needle (M) was fitted and a further set of performance figures taken. A small improvement was noted. The next step was to make some modifications to the carburettor piston. First, the transfer hole, which faces the engine, was threaded and blocked with a brass screw which was then filed flush and staked so that it would not loosen. Next, two new transfer holes were drilled in the base of the piston. The needle was changed to an E3 and the damper was modified by removing $\frac{1}{32}$in from the end to give a quicker lift to the piston.

G

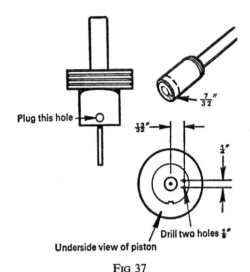

Plug this hole

$\frac{7}{32}''$

$1\frac{3}{32}''$

$\frac{1}{4}''$

Drill two holes $\frac{1}{8}''$

Underside view of piston

FIG 37

The quick-lift piston modifications made to a Mini
carburettor prior to fitting an E3 needle

As can be seen from the tables, the results were better from
the performance angle, although the fuel consumption suffered
compared with the M needle. For the E3 test, the paper element
air filter was removed. It had been left in place for the EB and
M needle tests. The next test was the fitting of a single Stromberg 150 CD carburettor which went on to the standard inlet
manifold using an adaptor plate. This carburettor is normally
recommended for Minis which have had some cylinder-head
modification, so it was perhaps unfair to expect impressive
results when bolted to a standard 848cc engine. Before fitting, the
carburettor flange hole in the intake manifold and hole in the
throttle cable plate were enlarged to 1½in diameter. There was
a perceptible improvement compared with the E3.

Fitting a straight-through silencer to the same car in addition
to the Stromberg CD gave a slight additional gain at higher
speeds.

Mini: Carburettor Comparisons

Acceleration from rest	Standard	SU, M needle, filter cartridge	SU, E3 needle, no cartridge	Stromberg CD 150 no filter	Straight-through silencer
0–30mph	6·0sec	5·5sec	5·4sec	4·9sec	4·9sec
0–40mph	9·9sec	9·5sec	9·1sec	8·2sec	7·9sec
0–50mph	17·6sec	16·2sec	15·5sec	14·5sec	13·5sec
0–60mph	28·3sec	28·3sec	24·9sec	22·0sec	20·7sec
Fuel consumption at steady speeds					
30mph		58·8mpg	54·0mpg	57·2mpg	
40mph		49·6mpg	46·5mpg	48·8mpg	
50mph		45·4mpg	40·7mpg	42·6mpg	
60mph		37·0mpg	34·5mpg	36·3mpg	
Overall		44·4mpg	39·2mpg	34·0mpg	

Fish Carburettors There are two manufacturers of the Fish carburettor in Britain, but the principle of operation of the carburettor is the same in each case.

The Fish is unusual in that it does not have a choke and the fuel is discharged into the ingoing airstream through a number of drillings in the throttle spindle—a system that gives excellent atomisation of the fuel. Both manufacturers claim that the improved mixing of petrol and air enables the Fish carburettor to give an all-round improvement in power coupled with an improvement in fuel consumption, and independent test figures bear this out.

Fuel metering on the Fish is achieved by a pick-up arm attached to the throttle spindle. A drilling in the end of the arm passes over a graduated groove submerged in petrol. At small throttle openings, the groove is narrow and shallow permitting only a small quantity of fuel to pass to the metering holes in the spindle. But as the throttle is opened, the arm moves over the deeper, wider section of the groove and the fuel flow in the spindle increases.

The chamber in which the arm operates is alongside the float chamber and separated from it by a metal diaphragm. Holes in the diaphragm allow the fuel level in both chambers to be the same. In order to provide a richer mixture when the throttle is suddenly opened, a one-way leaf valve is fitted to the fuel entry hole in the diaphragm, ahead of the pick-up arm. When the throttle is snapped open, the pick-up arm displaces the fuel ahead of it, shuts the leaf, and forces a richer shot of petrol through the spindle holes.

There is a knack in tuning the Fish carburettor for best results (see Chapter 7) and there is also a knack in starting up from cold. Since the Fish has no separate choke, a rich mixture for starting is introduced into the inlet manifold by pumping the accelerator two or three times while operating the starter. The engine will usually fire readily, but the accelerator usually needs a regular 'blip' to keep the engine running on tick-over during the first few minutes—a procedure which may not appeal to less skilful drivers.

There is another problem which besets the Fish. In certain atmospheric conditions, particularly just after a cold start, it ices up. The carburettor's first-class atomisation system is to blame for this, since the fine spray of petrol in cold, damp air encourages frost to form at the throttle spindle, and this eventually blocks the discharge holes. When this happens the car mis-fires and stops. Waiting for about two minutes allows the heat of the engine to melt the ice, after which the engine often runs satisfactorily for the remainder of the journey. The condition can often be overcome by fitting a radiator blind or by fitting a heater in the choke tube.

Fixed-choke Carburettors Motor manufacturers who do not fit SU or Stromberg CD carburettors nearly always use a fixed-choke unit. Reduced to its crudest form, this has a float chamber and a main jet through which fuel passes to an outlet in the choke tube. The outlet is at the same level as the fuel in the float chamber. When the engine is running, the airstream through the choke tube draws fuel from the outlet and mixes it with the ingoing air.

So much for principles. The modern fixed-jet carburettors have more than a main jet. Depending on the type, they have idling jets, pilot jets, progression jets, air correction jets, emulsion tubes that mix fuel and air, accelerator pumps that squirt

neat fuel into the choke when the accelerator is pressed, economy
devices that weaken the mixture on light engine loads—all
geared to the job of providing the correct mixture at the right
time.
Once the jet settings have been arrived at, there is no adjustment on a fixed-choke carburettor other than for the idling
mixture and throttle opening. And this is why tuning shops
like them, for once they are set up with the right jetting, you
get a guaranteed level of performance.
The most popular fixed-choke carburettor for modified
engines is the Weber, although the Dellorto and Nikki are
emerging as alternatives. All these manufacturers make a twin-
choke horizontal carburettor which is ideal for competition
purposes and *can* be used on the road, providing you are gentle
with the throttle at low rpm. But a better alternative for road
use is a twin-choke progressive carburettor similar to the type
Ford first fitted to the Cortina GT. This could almost be described as a split-personality carburettor, because up to about
half-throttle only one choke operates and the engine can be
driven gently and economically.
Once past the half-throttle position, the butterfly in the second
choke begins to open—and the carburettor gearing makes it
open twice as fast as the first one. This sudden doubling of the
carburettor size gives a big improvement in acceleration at
highish revs in the intermediate gears, while with both chokes
fully open the top speed generally shows a marked increase.
These carburettors are usually sold complete with a manifold
as bolt-on kits for engines which do not readily accept twin SU
or Stromberg sets. Sometimes they are offered instead of twin
carburettors, and an engine occasionally performs better with
one progressive twin-choke than with a pair of variable-choke
units. It is not immediately apparent why this is so, for one
would expect two separate carburettors to give a better mixture
distribution to four cylinders than a twin-choke feeding into
one intake hole in the inlet manifold.
The only valid reason seems to be that the Weber, in par-

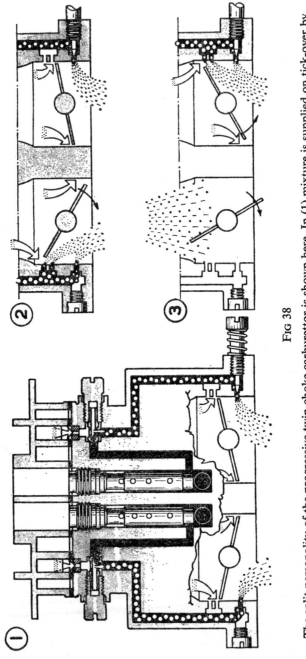

Fig 38

The split personality of the progressive twin-choke carburettor is shown here. In (1) mixture is supplied on tick-over by two idling feeds down-stream of the throttle butterflies. In (2) the accelerator pedal has been pressed a little and the primary throttle has begun to open, drawing its initial fuel supply from the progression holes. In (3) at about half travel on the accelerator pedal, the secondary choke begins to open. At full throttle, both chokes are fully open

ticular, produces a better mixture of petrol and air than the SU or Stromberg. If you look into the workings of the carburettors you can see why. The variable-choke units use a needle working in a jet to meter the fuel flow. The petrol is dragged out of the gap between the needle and the sides of the jet and some of it is drawn as fairly large globules into the inlet manifold.

The Weber, in common with some others, first mixes the fuel and air in an emulsion tube, and then the mixture goes to a discharge orifice inside a separate small venturi mounted in the centre of the choke tube. The atomisation with this set-up is a good deal better, and on a good inlet manifold this can more than compensate for the distribution advantage of two separate carburettors.

The other advantage of a progressive twin-choke is that, once properly jetted, it does not need to be balanced—a big scoring point with dissatisfied twin carburettor users. On the other hand, despite its progressive action, it tends to be less economical in use than twin-variable-choke units, presumably because most drivers use both chokes most of the time.

Cylinder Heads

Let us first look at what you can do yourself, and some of the ways and means of doing it.

A general clean-up is well within the capabilities of anyone who can do a 'de-coke' and has a power drill. All that is involved is removal of the cylinder head and the valves, then cleaning-up of all casting roughness in the inlet and exhaust ports. Of the two, the inlet ports are worth spending the most time on since a good finish here will produce the greatest increase.

To clean up the surface, you need a set of what tool-shops call mounted points—small rotary grindstones of varying shapes fixed to the end of a steel rod. These will enable you to clean up the entry of the inlet ports, although the length of the rod that goes in the drill chuck may not go in as far as the valve throat. It is possible to get over this by working through the valve hole from the combustion chamber end, but take care that the grindstone does not inadvertently chop a piece from the valve seat. For if this happens the valve cannot be ground in and it may be necessary to have a valve seat insert fitted, which is quite a performance.

Once most of the rough finish has been smoothed down, the surface can be polished with emery cloth. To hold the emery, take a ¼in bolt about 5in long, hacksaw off the head and with the bolt held upright in a vice, cut a slit down the middle about 1in deep. Put the bolt (slit outermost) in the drill, tear off a strip of 1in wide emery, engage it in the slit and wind it round the bolt. Assuming that you have put the emery in the right way round, you now have a gadget for polishing the ports to a shiny finish.

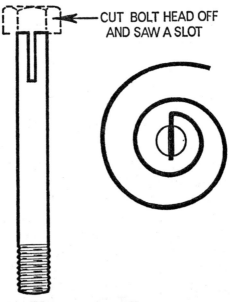

Fig 39

Port polisher—a bolt modified to carry a strip of emery cloth

The next thing to do is to match the head ports with those in the manifold. Until people like BLMC began making inlet manifold gaskets that fitted anything from an 850cc Mini to a Cooper 'S', you could reckon to open the ports on both manifold and head until they conformed with the gasket holes. Now I am not so sure that this method is infallible, so the safe thing to do is to take a strip of card from an old corn-flakes' packet or something similar, cut holes in it so it fits the head manifold studs *exactly*, write 'manifold' on the side facing you, and then use the ball end of a ball-pein hammer on the card to gently hammer round the edges of the inlet ports. Cut these out accurately.

Now put the side of the card marked 'manifold' the same way up against the inlet manifold. There are two possibilities here. Either the holes you carefully cut in the card are bigger than those in the manifold, in which case you scribe round them and leave a permanent record on the manifold, or the holes in the card are *smaller* than the corresponding ones in the manifold, in which event you take the hammer in your hand and carefully hammer round the edges to enlarge the holes in the card. Now transfer the card back on to the head and scribe round the edges of the holes.

Either way, you will end up with one set of holes that need enlarging to make the inlet manifold and the head a perfect step-free fit, and the appropriate ones should be enlarged to the scribed lines using a grindstone, or a rotary steel cutter on aluminium inlets, finishing with emery as before.

There are, of course, exceptions. It is not necessary to do this, for instance, where the manifold is located to the head by small sleeves that positively line up the inlet with the head ports. It should not be necessary on dowelled manifolds either, since the reason they are dowelled is to stop the ports getting out of line.

The reason for suggesting the use of a steel cutter on aluminium is that this soft metal clogs grindstones very quickly. In fact, even professional tuners find it difficult to get a clean finish on aluminium when polishing ports, so do not be too worried if the finish is not mirror-like. Just try and make it as smooth as possible, if necessary hand-finishing with oiled wet-or-dry paper on a piece of old broom handle. And while we are on the subject of inlet manifolds, do not forget to check the match at the carburettor end, opening up the manifold as necessary. Do not do any grinding on the carburettor.

Compression Ratio If we can ignore bowl-in-piston engines for a moment and concentrate on heads with integral combustion chambers, we now come to the stage where you can decide whether or not to have the compression ratio raised. Most engineering shops will surface-grind a head face reasonably cheaply. Some will usually suggest how much metal to take off to give a specific compression ratio, although few will guarantee the result.

There are one or two points to be allowed for before this work is done. The first is whether or not you can afford to risk the head being ruined. With small increases in compression, say involving the removal of up to ·040in from the head face, the risk is slight—but it is still there. Sometimes complications set in. For instance, on BLMC 'A' Series engines head grinding sometimes uncovers the oil feed gallery to the rockers which runs parallel to the head face. If this happens, the channel must be enlarged, fitted with a new tube to take the oil, and then brazed up again—and brazing cast-iron is no simple job.

One other snag to private ventures into the compression-raising field is that specific data are not usually available from the motor manufacturers—who, in general, heartily disapprove of surface-grinding cylinder heads. But as a rough guide, on pushrod overhead valve engines you can reckon that the average cylinder head can stand about ·060in off the head face without ill effects. Like the car manufacturers, I cannot guarantee this, unfortunately, but let us say that the risk of catastrophe is small. This rule does not apply to overhead camshaft heads. Removing large amounts of metal from the Hillman Imp, for instance, lowers the camshaft sprocket and affects the valve timing.

If you have not been put off, the next step is to decide on the

compression ratio you want. British five-star petrol allows
compression ratios of 10:1 to be used on cast-iron heads, and
about one ratio higher on aluminium heads. I would not recommend going any higher for road use. In fact, if you are
sticking to my recommended ·060in maximum, you will
probably find that this limits you to an increase of about one
ratio above standard. To find out the exact amount that must
be shaved off a given cylinder head, some measurement and
calculation is called for.

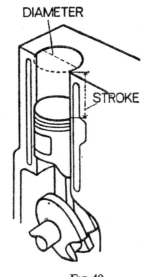

FIG 40

The two measurements required when calculating
the volume of the bore

Assume a compression ratio of 10:1 is required. The first
step is to measure the stroke of the piston with the piston at
BDC, and the diameter of the bore. The formula for calculating
the swept volume is piston stroke × diameter^2 × 0·7854. Let us
say that this comes to 252cc.

You must now calculate the volume of combustion chamber
needed to give 10:1 compression. The formula for this is:

$$Cv = \frac{Sv}{R-1}$$

Here, Cv = combustion chamber volume, Sv = the swept volume of the bore and R = the ratio required.

Substituting the figures we get:

$$Cv = \frac{252}{10-1} = \frac{252}{9} = 28cc$$

This 28cc will, of course, include the volume taken up by the head gasket and the volume of any depressions or cut-outs in the piston. If the gasket hole is circular, the volume can be calculated. If it is an irregular shape, trace it on metric graph paper, count the squares and calculate from this. The volume of, say, a dished piston, can be measured by filling it with a paraffin/ oil mix from a burette.

Let us assume that the gasket space takes up 2cc and the piston depressions 2cc. These are subtracted from 28 to give 24cc—the volume required in the combustion chamber alone.

You are now at the stage to determine how much metal comes off the head face. With the head upside-down and level, and the valves and plugs in, measure 24cc of paraffin/oil mixture from a burette into the combustion chamber. Now, using a depth gauge, measure between the head face and the surface in the centre of the puddle. This is the depth of metal that must be removed to give 10:1 compression.

Once you know this system there is nothing to stop you from re-shaping the combustion chambers to what you think is a racing profile, if you want to, and using the above method to get the desired compression ratio afterwards. This, in fact, is what the tuning shops do. There are one or two snags to this, though. The first is that combustion chamber reshaping, particularly for road use, is a scientific business where the best results are arrived at after considerable flow testing, so uneducated carving may possibly do more harm than good.

Secondly, the more metal you remove from the combustion chambers, the more must be ground from the cylinder-head face to get back a reasonable compression ratio. On some engines, removing a big thickness from the head face will cause unwelcome side-effects—such as the valves hitting the block or pistons.

If you have a burette, there is, however, one check that is worth making on the combustion chambers while the head is on the bench. Set it up level with the valves and plugs in, and measure the volume of each combustion chamber. It sometimes helps if a sheet of Perspex with a hole drilled in it is placed over the chamber, since this indicates exactly when it is full. Ideally, the chambers should not vary by more than 0·2cc. If they do, grind metal from the smaller chambers until they are all equal in volume to the biggest one.

Spark Plugs Raising the compression will inevitably increase combustion temperatures when the engine is running, and it may be necessary to go to one grade 'colder' spark plugs to prevent pre-ignition.

FIG 41

A 'hot' plug (*left*) has a longer insulator nose compared with a 'cold' one

If it seems strange that hotter engines need cold plugs, the theory behind it is that the heat-range of a plug is determined by the length of the ceramic insulator nose which surrounds the centre electrode. The hottest part of the plug is the top of the insulator, and the only way this heat can dissipate itself is by travelling along the insulator until it comes to the point where it seats on the metal shell. So plugs with long insulator noses retain their heat longer and are known as hot plugs, whereas short insulator nose plugs run cooler and are cold plugs. For increases in compression of one ratio, it may not be necessary to change the plugs at all. But, if in doubt, do some high-speed runs and check plug condition as detailed in Chapter 7. If the plug ends have a glazed look, you may need one grade colder.

Ignition Timing An increase in compression ratio means that the ignition timing does not normally require so much static advance. With an increase of one ratio, best results are usually obtained by retarding the static ignition setting 2–4 degrees. This can be checked on the road (see Chapter 7).

The following table suggests a number of possible 'Stage 1' conversions for popular British cars. I have tried to keep to inexpensive modifications which will not turn the car into a track-burner, but which will give it a little more zip for overtaking and usually a slightly increased top speed as well. All modifications are of the 'bolt-on' type and do not require much engine dismantling. Where they are numbered, this indicates the order of improvements, those with higher numbers can be added at a later date if required.

Stage One Modifications

British Leyland

All the former BMC cars are fitted with SU carburettors, and where a single one is fitted, changing to a twin SU layout generally gives a power improvement of about 10 per cent. The simplest way to get twin SUs is to obtain a suitable manifold and linkage, buy one new SU and join it to the old one. This works well where the existing carburettor is in good condition. If it is badly worn, you are better off with two new carburettors.

Other carburettors, like twin Stromberg CDs, Webers and the
Fish, work well on these engines, but since the engines come
equipped with SUs, most people stick to them. Engines
already fitted with twin SUs benefit by going up one carburettor
size, but since this involves throwing away the existing units,
most people leave this swap until the engine has covered a good
mileage.

Mini 848cc, 1000cc 1100 and 1300 (not automatic)	(1) Single 1½in or twin 1¼in SUs. (2) Modify cylinder head. (3) Fit three-branch exhaust manifold, straight-through silencer.
Mini-Coopers, including 'S', Sprite/Midget 1098cc– 1275cc, twin-carburettor 1100s and 1300s	(1) Twin 1½in SUs. (2) Modify cylinder head. (3) Fit three-branch exhaust manifold and straight-through silencer.
Austin Maxi 1500 and 1750	(1) Twin 1½in SUs. (2) Four-branch exhaust manifold and straight-through silencer.
Austin/Morris 1800	(1) Twin 1¾in SUs. (2) Modify head. (3) Fit three-branch exhaust and straight- through silencer.
MGB	(1) Twin 2in SUs. (2) Modify cylinder head.

Chrysler/Rootes

The most popular cars here with the engine tuners are the
Hillman Imps. They already have what should be a highly-
efficient overhead camshaft light alloy engine, but the makers
have purposely restricted the breathing by fitting a small carburettor and an inlet manifold which has the same shape as a
garden rake. Best initial results come from improved carburation, and a variety of conversions are available using progressive
twin-choke carburettors, twin SUs or twin Strombergs, with
possibly twin Strombergs being the favourites, since Chrysler
fit these on the Sunbeam Imp Sport and Stiletto engines. The
Avenger is comparatively new to the tuning shops, so the car-

buration suggestion is a guess on my part. The medium-car range, which have single carburettors, the twin-choke Solex compound carburettor or twin fixed-choke Zenith carburettors benefit from twin Strombergs.

Imp/Chamois 875cc single carburettor	(1) Twin 1¼in Stromberg CDs. (2) Four-branch exhaust system.
Sunbeam Imp Sport and Stiletto	(1) Modify cylinder head and change carburettor needles. (2) Four-branch exhaust system.
Hillman Avenger 1250 and 1500	(1) Twin 1½in Stromberg CDs. (2) Modify cylinder head.
Hillman Minx, Humber Sceptre, Singer Gazelle, Vogue, Sunbeam Rapier, and Alpine (all with upright 1725cc engines)	(1) Twin 1½in Stromberg CDs or a single 28/36 DCD Weber. (2) Four-branch exhaust manifold. (3) Modify cylinder head.
Hillman Hunter, Sunbeam Rapier, Vogue, Alpine, Humber Sceptre and Hillman GT (with canted 1725cc engines)	(1) Modify cylinder head.
Hillman Minx and Singer Gazelle (1496cc)	(1) Twin 1½in Stromberg CDs. (2) Four-branch exhaust manifold. (3) Modify cylinder head.

Ford

This company already produces high-performance GT options for its small and medium saloon car ranges, and where the engine size is not being altered Ford concentrates on a camshaft change, the use of a progressive twin-choke Weber carburettor and a four-branch exhaust manifold. These modifications can be applied to the engines in the more basic saloons, and this is what most tuning organisations do. The position regarding head modifications became difficult when Ford introduced the cross-flow, four-cylinder engine used in the Escort, Capri and the later Mark 2 Cortinas, since these engines are of the bowl-in-piston type and, except for the GT variants, have

completely flat cylinder-head faces. This means that changing
the compression ratio involves either a change of pistons or
machining the existing pistons and the top face of the block—
too much effort for a mild stage of tune.

The Ford Vee engines are also of the bowl-in-piston type. I
have dealt here only with the Corsair, since there is little demand
for extra performance from the Zephyr and Zodiac.

Anglia 105E, Mk1 Cortina 1200 and 1500 (these have combustion chambers in the cylinder head)	(1) Twin-choke progressive 28/36 Weber DCD carburettor or similar on Cortina GT-type inlet manifold. (2) Cylinder head modifications. (3) Four-branch exhaust.
Cortina GT 1500	(1) Modify cylinder head.
Escort 1100, 1300 Super, Cortina 1300 and 1600 Mk2	(1) Twin-choke progressive 28/36 Weber or Fish carburettor. (2) Four-branch exhaust.
Escort 1300 GT, Capri 1300 GT, 1600 GT and Cortina 1600 GT Mk2	(1) Enlarge and re-jet existing 32 DFE Weber carburettor. (2) Clean-up and enlarge ports in cylinder head.
Corsair V4 1700cc	(1) Fish carburettor.

Triumph

From the engine tuner's angle, Triumph engines are noted
for the great variety of carburettors they use. Depending on the
car, it may have a one fixed-choke down-draught carburettor,
twin SUs, twin Strombergs or—on the British version of the
TR6 and 2·5 PI—Lucas fuel injection.

With no obvious guide lines, the carburation situation can
become confused. It may seem strange, for instance, to swap
twin 1¼in SUs on the Triumph 1300 TC for a different twin-
carb manifold and a pair of twin 1½in Stromberg CDs. However, to some extent one is governed by what is available. If it
is any consolation, the latest HS-Type 1½in SU would not fit
the standard twin-carburettor manifold anyway.

H

Herald 948, 1200, 12/50 and Spitfire Mk1 and 2	(1) Four-branch exhaust system with twin 1¼in Stromberg CDs. Where further tuning is considered, fit twin 1½in Strombergs. (2) Modify cylinder head.
Herald 13/60 and Triumph 1300	(1) Twin 1½in Stromberg CDs (use one extra carburettor in conjunction with existing unit). (2) Four-branch exhaust manifold. (3) Modify head.
Spitfire Mk3 and Triumph 1300 TC	(1) Twin 1½in Stromberg CDs. (2) Modify head. (3) Four-branch exhaust manifold.
Vitesse 1600	(1) Twin 1¼in Stromberg CDs. If further tuning is considered, fit twin 1½in Strombergs. (2) Modify cylinder head.
Vitesse 2000, Triumph GT6 and Triumph 2000	(1) Twin 1¾in Stromberg CDs or three 1½in Stromberg CDs—this allows use of the existing twin 1½in units with one new carburettor and revised manifolding. (2) Six-branch exhaust system. (3) Modify cylinder head.
Triumph TR3–4	(1) Four-branch extractor exhaust manifold. (2) Modify cylinder head.
Triumph 2·5 PI and TR6	(1) Six-branch exhaust manifold. (2) Modify cylinder head.

Vauxhall

Vauxhall Motors does not itself go in for engine modifications and this has resulted in few tuning kits being available for this marque compared with some others. In standard form, Vauxhall engines use either a single down-draught, fixed-choke carburettor, a single Stromberg CD, or twin Stromberg CDs. The tuning kits that are available generally substitute a progressive twin-choke down-draught carburettor, usually the D 28/32 Nikki for small engines, and the larger D 32/35 where more performance is needed. The 28/36 Weber can also be used.

| Viva HA, HB, HC, 1600 and Victor 1600 (economy tune) | (1) Twin-choke Nikki D28/32. (2) Free-flow exhaust manifold. (3) Modify cylinder head. |
| Victor 2000, Viva GT and Victor 1600 (performance tune) | (1) Twin-choke Nikki D32/35. (2) Free-flow exhaust manifold. (3) Modify cylinder head. |

5
ADVANCED TUNING

A bolt-on carburettor conversion and some do-it-yourself porting and polishing of the cylinder head can normally be reckoned to give a power improvement of around 10 per cent over standard. If you want more than this you have to leave 'do-it-yourself' methods behind and put your engine in the hands of a professional engine tuner. What is done depends on the engine, the tuner and the contents of your wallet. For it is an undeniable fact that the more money you are prepared to spend, the more horsepower you can have.

There are three separate ways of going about advanced tuning. Firstly, you can leave the engine capacity as it is, but make it more efficient by comprehensive cylinder head modifications, the addition of bigger or more efficient carburettors, perhaps a change of camshaft and a number of other detailed internal alterations.

Alternatively, you can enlarge the engine's capacity. This can often be done by boring it out or changing the crankshaft for one with a longer throw—or both. Where this is not possible, it may be feasible to get rid of the existing engine altogether and substitute a bigger one.

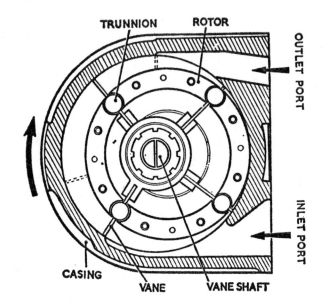

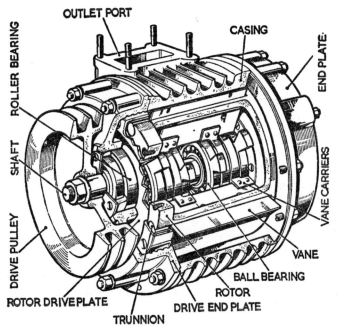

FIG 42

Allard-Shorrock supercharger in section: the rotor turns the vanes
which have a very small clearance between their tips and the casing.
The cutaway of the same unit shows the heavy-duty bearings which
support the rotor and vane shaft

The third possibility is the easiest of all. And that is super-charging. Among motor club members, who probably make up the largest group of customers for the engine tuners, super-charging is not popular because supercharged competition cars get something of a raw deal in the rules covering club com-petitions, where it is common for supercharged cars to be made to run in the next-highest capacity class. And this can mean that a supercharged 1150cc engined-car has to compete against vehicles with normally aspirated engines of 1600cc or more. But if you are not interested in one specific class of motor sport, adding a supercharger is one of the quickest ways of increasing the power output by about 30 per cent without making any other modifications at all.

In basic terms, a supercharger is a compressor or air pump. It fits between the carburettor and the engine's inlet manifold and is belt-driven by the engine crankshaft. The theory that it works upon is simple: a normally aspirated engine draws in the petrol/air mixture at atmospheric pressure, which is 14·74psi. What a supercharger does is to increase this pressure. Most road-going ones work at around 5psi, a pressure approximately one-third greater than atmospheric.

The effect of force-feeding the mixture into the engine by this amount is to increase the weight of mixture in the engine on the intake stroke by 33 per cent, and this has the happy result of providing a power increase in the region of 33 per cent. In some instances, the results are even better. Allard-Shorrock, the firm which makes the most widely used British super-charger, says that one of its installations gives more than 50 per cent improvement on the VW 1200 engine. It is known that the flat-four VW has one of the longest and, from the power angle, one of the most inefficient inlet manifolds in the business. Supercharging this engine, therefore, not only crams in 33 per cent more mixture, but also cancels out the inefficiencies of the inlet manifold which hampers the performance in un-modified form.

If you examine the power curves of a standard engine with

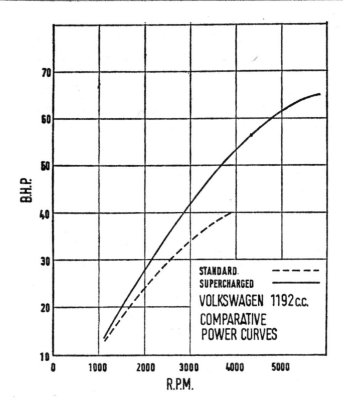

FIG 43

VW 1200 power graph

and without a supercharger, you will see that on the supercharged version the improved output is noticeable from about
2,000rpm onwards; in other words, there is an all-round improvement in power. In practice, this means that there is better
top-gear acceleration from moderate engine speeds. The improvement can be likened to increasing the engine capacity by
one-third—thus a supercharged 1500cc engine behaves like an
unsupercharged 2 litre power unit.

You do not get a power-step-up like this for nothing, of
course. If the supercharger is pushing more mixture into the

engine, for a start the fuel consumption is going to rise. Allard-Shorrock says that there need be no increase in fuel consumption if the car is driven 'without taking advantage of the increased power . . .'. But if you were going to do that you would not have fitted the supercharger in the first place. Using the extra performance, the firm says, increases consumption by 10–15 per cent, which in mpg terms means that you could

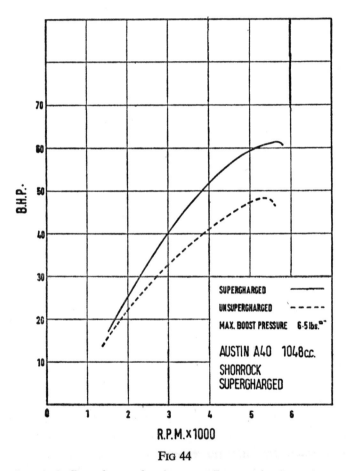

FIG 44

A typical effect of supercharging a small car engine is to give a noticeable increase in power from as low as 2,000rpm

expect 25½–27mpg from a supercharged car which in unsupercharged form did 30mpg. In addition, 100 octane petrol should be used.

Another by-product is that the combustion chamber temperatures are higher on a supercharged engine, and this means that the cooling system has more heat to dissipate. Providing the radiator and the water galleries in the block and cylinder head are in good order, this should present no problem, although in cars where continuous high speeds are envisaged it would be advisable to fit an oil cooler.

On old engines, I would not suggest fitting a supercharger without first giving the power unit a complete overhaul. This may sound drastic, but look at it this way—to get a 33 per cent step-up in power on the same engine by any other means inevitably involves some dismantling. When this is done, it is normal practice to examine any suspect components and renew them if necessary. The end product is then an engine with sufficient strength to withstand the increased power. A supercharger, on the other hand, is just bolted on. There is no engine dismantling involved, so there is nothing to stop you bolting it on to, say, a rather tired 850cc engine which has done 80,000 miles and lacks oil pressure. The effect of a supercharger on this would be to finish it off very quickly. A 33 per cent power increase also means an equivalent extra load on the crankshaft, its bearings, the con-rods and pistons.

Increased Capacity

The oldest trick in the book when it comes to increasing the power output is simply to make the engine a little bigger. At just about every motor show, some manufacturer will turn up with a face-lifted version of a standard saloon, with a bit more power—and a slightly bigger engine capacity. Over the years, the BMC 'A' Series engine has increased in capacity from 848cc to 1275cc, and the equivalent Standard-Triumph engine, which began life powering the Standard Eight with 848cc, has similarly grown to 1296cc.

There are two ways of increasing the capacity of an engine. Either you increase the diameter of the bore by boring it out, or you increase the stroke of the piston so that it goes further down the bore. At first sight, boring-out seems the easiest, for all you need are oversize pistons of the appropriate dimensions and a tame engineer to do an oversize rebore job for you.

The amount of metal that can be removed when boring out a block is governed by the proximity of the water galleries. Unfortunately, it is not even necessary to break through into a water channel to make a hash-up of enlarging the bores, for if the casting is particularly thin in one place it may become porous—then water will get in, the exhaust gas will get out, and you will have an engine that boils up frequently and consumes its water at the same time, which can be very puzzling. One way over the problem of porous blocks is to over-bore them, if necessary cutting right into the water channels, and then press in a liner. This is then bored to the required size. This method is sometimes necessary when the Ford 1500cc block is bored out to 1650cc, while Hartwell uses a similar method, but with wet liners, to increase the capacity of the Imp from 875cc to 998cc.

Increasing Stroke This system involves changing the crankshaft and connecting-rods, but very often the same pistons can be used. Its advantage over boring-out is that it is purely a question of changing mechanical parts and, except where clearance must be provided for the longer-throw crankshafts, no machining is involved.

In case you are wondering how increasing the stroke manages to get the piston to go further down the bore, but prevents it coming out the top, the answer is that shorter con-rods are used with the longer-throw crank. The con-rod length is arranged so that the piston crown is level with the top of the bore at TDC, and the extra throw of the crank draws it further down the bore at BDC.

Ford designed its overhead valve 997cc Anglia, Cortina 1200cc and Classic 1340cc engines with a similar block casting and the same diameter pistons. The different capacities were obtained by changing the crankshafts and con-rods, and by fitting the appropriate parts an Anglia can be enlarged to 1340cc. In addition the heads were altered, since an Anglia-size combustion chamber on a 1340cc engine gave a compression ratio of around 12:1. The popular modification when enlarging the Anglia to 1340cc is to rework its combustion chambers, which improves the gas-flow and at the same time brings the compression ratio to a more reasonable figure.

Increasing the stroke obviously depends on the availability from the manufacturer of a longer-throw crankshaft which is interchangeable with the original. Where one cannot be found, or the work involved is too costly, there are two alternatives. Either do some advanced modifying on the existing engine, or fit a different engine altogether.

Advanced Modifications

The most advanced tuning of all is found on racing engines, where the average small capacity unit may be producing more than twice the power of an equivalent engine in a road car. But the way the racing engine produces its power is almost exactly opposite to the way the power is produced in the family car. On the family saloon, the engine delivers useful power from about 1,500rpm—about 20-25mph in top gear—right up to a maximum of around 5,000rpm, at which stage the output begins to fall off because the engine 'runs out of breath', either because of limitations in the valve size or the camshaft, or because valve float (bounce) has set in. The racing engine, on the other hand, probably produces virtually nothing below 4,000-5,000rpm, but from this point on a great deal of power is available up to the engine's maximum rpm, which is possibly 8,000-9,000rpm.

Racing cars are expected to make one standing start per

race, so despite the effect of slipping the clutch and feeding in the power with the engine turning at 5,000rpm or so, there is every likelihood that the clutch will survive for at least one racing season. On the road, it probably would not survive the rigours of traffic 'stop-start' driving for more than a week. So, for road use, full-race-tuned engines are not to be recommended. Instead, it is better to aim for slightly less maximum power but to get more of it at lower rpm. This involves building in some flexibility, and you end up with something nearer the stage of tune used on a rally car.

Unlike Stage One, where the accent was on ease of fitting, simplicity and cheapness, advanced tuning requires that the engine be treated as a whole. The reason for this is that where modifications are being made to boost the power output by perhaps 50 per cent or more, some standard components cannot stand the strain. If these are not strengthened it is possible, for instance, to get a situation where the extra power from a sophisticated cylinder head and advanced carburation cannot be used above 5,000rpm because the timing gears will break up.

So to maintain reliability on a heavily modified engine, it is advisable to take some anti-burst measures, and strengthen any components that are liable to break. This may take the form, for instance, of stiffening up the crankshaft main-bearing caps to discourage crankshaft whip, or the fitting of a stiffer crankshaft. In fact, all suspect moving parts that have a known tendency to fail if overloaded should be strengthened or replaced by stronger components. If we can re-cap to a racing engine for a moment; if you took, say, a full-race-tuned Escort 1300 engine apart, you would find that virtually all the standard Escort moving parts had been replaced by stronger components.

Another reason for treating the engine as a whole in the higher stages of tuning is that big alterations in one department will only work satisfactorily if a comparable alteration has been made elsewhere. For example, on its own, a high-compression big-valve cylinder head with enlarged porting will probably give worse performance if bolted to an otherwise standard engine.

But used in conjunction with big carburettors, a modified camshaft and a straight-through exhaust system, it would show a big increase. I have itemised under separate headings some of the more popular methods of extracting a lot of extra power from an engine without increasing its capacity. The modifications are dealt with separately because this is the most straightforward way of presenting them in book form. For best results, they should, as I have already mentioned, be used in conjunction with other improvements.

Carburation The carburettor arrangements described so far are suitable for quite advanced tuning. But for maximum power, the best carburettor set-up is typified by the Weber DCOE series of horizontal twin-choke carburettors. The most popular sizes are the 40 DCOE and the 45 DCOE, the number referring to the diameter of the carburettor bore at the throttle butterfly in millimetres.

The DCOE has even better mixture-producing capabilities than the down-draught twin-choke, and because the chokes on the horizontal carburettor are entirely separate, this means that on engines with one inlet port per cylinder, such as the small Fords, fitting a pair of twin-chokes will give each cylinder its own individual intake. This system is unquestionably better from the maximum power angle than using an intake manifold which feeds, say, all four cylinders—since a common manifold nearly always gives a different mixture strength to the centre two cylinders, compared with the two outside cylinders. On four-cylinder engines with only two inlet ports, a single twin-choke still gives best results compared with other twin-carburettor set-ups.

When it is properly jetted and choked, a horizontal twin-choke carburettor will give good pulling power from about 2,000rpm upwards, depending on the camshaft, with its best performance at full-throttle and high engine revolutions. Fuel consumption will depend on the other engine alterations, but it should not be excessive.

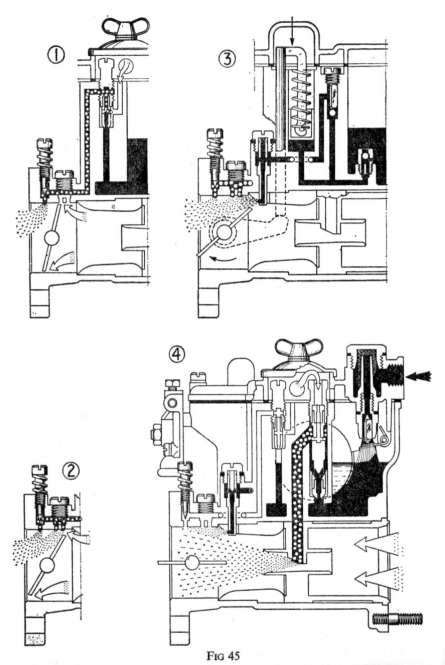

FIG 45

The DCOE twin-choke Weber carburettor draws fuel from a number of sources as the parallel throttles open. With the engine ticking over (1) an idling feed hole in each choke allows mixture into the intake immediately downstream of the throttle butterfly. As the butterfly opens (2) the progression holes supply more fuel which is drawn by the air-flow past the butterfly edge. If the throttle continues opening the accelerator pump (3) aims a richening shot down the intake before the transformation to full throttle (4) when the main jet assembly supplies fuel from the nozzle within the auxiliary venturi. Both chokes work simultaneously in this way

Unfortunately, if twin-choke horizontal carburettors are not set-up correctly for an engine, they can be something of a nuisance. The DCOE Weber, for instance, has a series of progression holes that allow a steadily increasing amount of fuel into the chokes during the first few degrees of throttle opening. But when the throttle butterfly passes a certain angle, the progression holes cease to operate and, by rights, the fuel supply from the main assembly takes over. To assist the smooth transition from the progression holes to main jet operation, the accelerator pump squirts a richening shot of petrol into each choke.

Now if the mixture from the main jet assembly is not quite right, an almost knife-edge situation exists at the point where the throttle butterfly leaves the progression holes behind and fuel begins to issue from the main jet assembly. If the main jet mixture is wrong, the engine will give a gasp and almost stop when this point is reached. The flat spot can be overcome by changing down a gear, when the increase in engine revolutions will step-up the airflow through the chokes and get the main jet assembly working.

At first sight it appears that you can overcome this situation by increasing the volume of the richening shot from the accelerator pump—in other words, fitting a bigger pump jet. This sometimes helps, but the fuel consumption gets worse. The real answer lies in the choice of the correct combination of chokes, emulsion tubes, main jets, air correction jets and pilot jets. With chokes and emulsion tubes costing around £1 a time (two per carburettor, remember) the chances of an amateur getting the jetting right without spending a small fortune are almost negligible.

Because these carburettors are critical to changes in engine specification (you may have to re-jet if a different camshaft were fitted) it pays, if you are going to use this sort of carburation, to get all the engine modifications done in one go, so that the carburettor settings can be right from the start. Besides Weber, Dellorto, Solex and Nikki also make twin-choke horizontal carburettors.

1

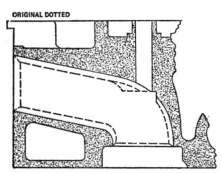

ORIGINAL DOTTED

COMPLETED INLET PORT MODIFICATION (BEFORE VALVE SEAT CUTTING)

2

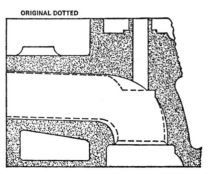

ORIGINAL DOTTED

COMPLETED EX. PORT MODIFICATION (BEFORE SEAT CUTTING)

3

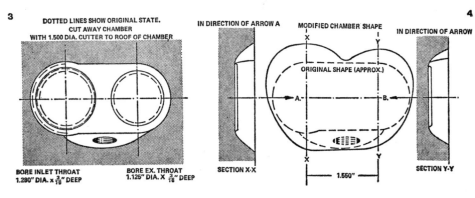

DOTTED LINES SHOW ORIGINAL STATE.
CUT AWAY CHAMBER
WITH 1.500 DIA. CUTTER TO ROOF OF CHAMBER

BORE INLET THROAT
1.280" DIA. x $\frac{3}{16}$" DEEP

BORE EX. THROAT
1.125" DIA. X $\frac{3}{16}$" DEEP

IN DIRECTION OF ARROW A

MODIFIED CHAMBER SHAPE

IN DIRECTION OF ARROW

ORIGINAL SHAPE (APPROX.)

A.

B.

SECTION X-X

1.550"

SECTION Y-Y

4

FIG 46

In the search for improved gas-flow and improved combustion, some heads are radically reworked. These diagrams refer to a Ford 105E Anglia head as modified to suit a Ford 1500cc block. The inlet port is enlarged to 1·156in diameter using reamers, after which the step at the base of the valve guide hole is blended into a curve. The exhaust port gets similar treatment, but grindstones can be used, since less metal is being removed. The combustion chamber is reshaped in two stages. First, a 1½in diameter cutter makes way for bigger inlet valves from a Ford Cortina 1500 GT. Next, the chamber is re-shaped to give a volume of 36cc. Using a head from a 997cc engine means, in this case, that no machining of the head face is required

Page 133 (*above*) Some need them, some don't—a 13 row oil cooler fitted to a Sprite; (*below*) heavy-duty suspension for a Ford Escort. The sheet metal parts on the left are to make up alternative upper rear shock absorber mountings so that the dampers operate vertically

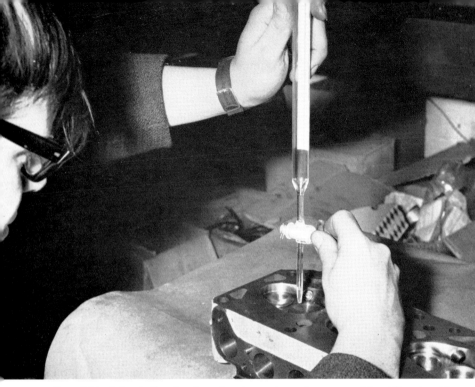

Page 134 (*above*) Combustion chamber volume is measured by filling it with fluid from a burette; (*below*) a Ford head modified for road use using a single twin-choke downdraught progressive carburettor (top) compared with a competition Ford head, ported and gas-flowed to take advantage of two twin-choke Weber carburettors

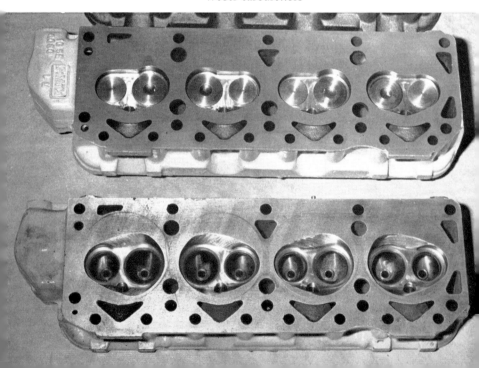

Fuel injection, where the fuel is accurately metered into each cylinder, gives better performance than any carburettors, but, on the distaff side, it is also a bit more expensive. The interesting fringe benefit of fuel injection is that because it does not rely on the airflow through the intake to atomise the fuel (the injector nozzles take care of this) a fuel-injected engine is a lot more flexible at low revolutions than one fitted with, say, a pair of twin-choke carburettors.

Cylinder Heads In conjunction with carburation improvements, advanced cylinder-head modification generally involves re-shaping the combustion chambers, where these are in the head, to give the maximum flow of the inlet charge past the valve; and, to this end, the inlet port is usually re-shaped and often the section under the valve head is enlarged. On some engines the valve guides are ground away in this area to give a regular valve throat profile. (See Figure 46.)

The size of the inlet valve is usually increased. As we have seen, this may give a little less power at low revolutions but gives a good deal extra at high engine speeds. The exhaust valve is sometimes enlarged and may be changed for a heavy-duty type which is better able to withstand high temperatures than the standard item. Re-shaping the combustion chambers naturally increases their volume and decreases the compression ratio, so as part of the treatment the head face is surface-ground, generally to give a fairly high ratio of perhaps 10:1 or above, and with this set-up it is normally expected that the car will run on 100 octane petrol.

Camshafts In the previous chapter I purposely avoided recommending a change of camshaft because this, above all else, can change the character of an engine entirely. It is the camshaft which is mainly responsible for the racing engine producing very little power below about 4,000rpm. And it is also the camshaft which enables it to burst into life above this speed. The camshaft controls the valves. Its profile determines the

I

precise moment when the inlet valve begins to open, the amount
it lifts off its seat, and the time it stays open.

It has already been shown that, by allowing for a small
amount of overlap when both the inlet and exhaust valves are
slightly open, the tail-end of the exhaust going out of the
cylinder can be used to draw in a little of the inlet charge. High-
performance camshafts exaggerate this, and increase the overlap
period. Holding both valves open a little longer means that there
is more time for the exhaust to act on the inlet charge and,
therefore, one should get more mixture into the cylinder on the
intake stroke. In fact, where increased power is the sole aim,
it is allowable for some of the inlet charge to come into the
cylinder and follow the exhaust gas straight past the exhaust
valve, on the basis that if the overlap is exerting this much pull
the remainder of the inlet charge will give greatly improved
cylinder filling. Fuel consumption will suffer, of course. There
is another advantage to losing some of the inlet charge in this
way, too: the stream of unburnt petrol/air mixture past the
exhaust valve helps to keep it cool.

One can tell the amount of valve overlap a camshaft gives by
looking at the camshaft timing figures. These figures indicate,
in degrees of crankshaft rotation, the point at which the cam-

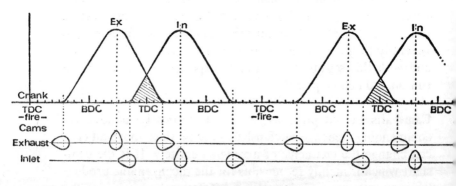

FIG 47

Camshaft overlap occurs at the end of the exhaust stroke and at the
beginning of the inlet cycle as this lift diagram shows

shaft opens and closes the valves. Normally, camshaft timing will be given like this: 25–65–65–25.

The first two figures refer to the inlet valve and the last two, the exhaust valve. Broken down further, they show that the inlet valve opens at 25° before TDC and closes 65° after BDC. The exhaust valve opens 65° BBDC and closes 25° ATDC. Since the intake stroke follows the exhaust stroke, the total valve overlap when the piston goes over TDC is 25 + 25 = 50°. This particular camshaft timing is used by Ford on the Escort GT in place of the standard camshaft. Combined with a modified cylinder head, it is said to give 10bhp more and yet allow the engine to remain tractable at low speeds.

The rally camshaft for the same engine is timed 45–80–83–40. The valve overlap in this case is bigger at 85°, and some low-speed power is sacrificed to gain more power in the mid-speed ranges and at maximum rpm. The camshaft recommended for racing on the same engine has a valve overlap of 106°, and is timed 53–86–86–53. This is not recommended for road use because it gives maximum power only in the higher rev-ranges.

The principle of increased lift is reasonably obvious. If you lift the valve up higher, more mixture can get through the hole that it uncovers. On a road-going engine there are limits to the amount of valve lift you can use. For a start, there are the obvious physical problems of the valve being lifted too much and hitting the piston or the block; there is also the possibility that the valve spring will compress up solid when the engine is running. The result of a 'solid' valve spring is to break up the rocker gear or drop the valve on top of the piston. Either can wreck an engine in a split-second. Where this is a possibility, camshaft suppliers usually recommend checking, when the engine is cold, that the valve can be moved, say, an extra ¹⁄₃₂in when it is on full lift with the correct valve gaps set.

On the majority of overhead valve engines, fitting a new camshaft involves taking the engine out, or at least a certain amount of major dismantling. When this is done, it is advisable to check the condition of the camshaft bearings and fit new cam

followers. On overhead camshaft engines like the Hillman Imp,
fitting a new camshaft calls for a good deal of work to obtain
the correct valve clearances. With this type of engine it is
generally a lot less trouble, if you are fitting the parts yourself,
to buy the camshaft already fitted to a modified cylinder head.

An alternative to a high-lift camshaft is a set of high-lift
rockers. So far as I know these, which are made by Speedwell,
are only available for BMC 'A' Series engines. The rockers have
the pivot point changed to alter the leverage and are fitted using
a modified set of rocker pillars. The effect of the rockers is to
give the valves extra lift while using the same camshaft. They
cannot, of course, alter the overlap.

Since a change of rocker gear only involves minor dismantling,
they have a particular appeal for enthusiasts who like to use
their road cars for weekend motor sport. Changing the rockers
at the weekend gives the car engine more top-end performance
at the expense of some flexibility at low revs, but the flexibility
can be restored by swapping the high-lift rockers for the
standard ones after the competition.

Anti-burst Measures All production-car engines have a built-in
margin of strength. But if you are increasing the load on these
by putting the power up by perhaps 50 per cent, or more, something is liable to break. What breaks first depends on the engine.
It could be the crankshaft, a con-rod, perhaps the timing gears,
or something unexpected like the end falling off the rocker shaft.
How much in the way of anti-burst treatment you have to give
your engine depends on how much extra power you are getting
from it. Some of the more popular measures are itemised below:

Crankshaft On the majority of British small-car engines built
after 1965, the crankshaft is pretty tough and for road tuning
it is not normally necessary to fit a stronger one. It is possible
to have the existing crankshaft 'Tuftrided', a process in which
the shaft is immersed in a salts bath at a temperature of 600°C
for several hours. The effect is to harden the surface (the depth

of penetration is sometimes as high as ⅛in) and to make the shaft 40–50 per cent stronger than an untreated one.

Main Bearings At high engine speeds there is a tendency for the crankshaft to whip, and in severe conditions this can break one of the main bearing caps. Stiffer caps are available to eliminate this. Either specially-made steel caps can be used, in which case they are normally line-bored in the block to suit the crankshaft, or, alternatively, there are sometimes stiffeners available for bolting across the outside of the existing caps.

Pistons Heavy-duty pistons may or may not be fitted, depending upon the stage of tune and the condition of the originals. Where high combustion-chamber temperatures and high revolutions are liable to be reached, a change of pistons is sometimes advisable. Competition-type pistons are made a fairly loose fit in the bores in order to discourage friction. This means there is a certain amount of piston-slap until the engine gets warm, and the oil consumption will be heavier than standard.

Con Rods The same remarks concerning crankshafts apply here. The Tuftriding process can be used providing the con-rods have not been bent and re-straightened.

Oil Pump Up-rated oil pumps are available for most engines. On competition engines, the crankshaft clearances are normally set up on the loose side, and an oil pump capable of delivering increased pressure is used. It should not be necessary on engines using standard road-going bearing clearances.

Balancing This does nothing for the power output, but reduces the vibration at high engine rpm. Normally, the crankshaft, flywheel and clutch pressure plate assembly are statically and dynamically balanced, and the weights of pistons and con rods equalised. Car manufacturers do, of course, balance the crankshaft and flywheel assembly during manufacture, but some improvement can be obtained by a specialist. When moving parts have been lightened re-balancing is, of course, essential.

Valve Gear It rather depends on the engine whether a breakage within the valve gear is imminent at high engine speeds. Minis, for instance, are known to chew the teeth of their timing sprockets if a combination of heavy-duty valve springs and high revs are used. Some other engines break their rocker shafts, others strip the teeth off the timing gears. Most engine tuners know the potential weaknesses of their chosen power units, so it is best to be guided by their experience.

Pulleys You may not, perhaps, think that you could over-rev a dynamo. But you can. A larger pulley and an alternative fan belt take care of matters here.

Fuel Pump A pair of twin-choke carburettors at full bore will undoubtedly consume more fuel than the standard vehicle. It may be necessary, therefore, to increase the delivery rate of the fuel pump. The most popular way of doing this is to fit an electric pump into the fuel system. If the car has a mechanical pump this can be removed, and the hole in the crankcase blanked off.

Flywheel Lightening the flywheel gives a much quicker pick-up from idling and fractionally speeds up the process of changing-down through the gearbox. For racing it is essential to reliability since lightening the flywheel helps prevent serious torsional vibration problems. On the road, the engine will idle more roughly and will be more liable to stall in traffic. I would not bother except for competition purposes.

Sump Baffling Putting baffles in the sump to prevent oil surge on corners is an essential if you are going to use the car for the occasional closed-circuit sprint. Where the sump is not already baffled, the normal method is to put a false floor in the sump a few inches above the bottom. Leave a hole big enough to get the oil pick-up pipe and strainer through. On Minis, which have a sump full of gears, a special anti-surge pick-up pipe is available from British Leyland Special Tuning.

Transmission Under this heading comes the clutch, gearbox, prop-shaft, differential and half-shafts, which must all be strong enough to cope with the extra power you are feeding into them. The clutch on the average car will normally put up with a reasonable increase in loading without protest. It is impossible to generalise on how much the standard production clutch will take, so be guided by the experts if in doubt. Heavy-duty clutch pressure plate assemblies and clutch discs are readily available from clutch manufacturers.

Gearboxes normally accept a substantial increase in power from the standard engine without trouble. However, some 'cooking' cars with their engines tuned close to the limit may also be reaching the limits of the gearbox. If this is happening, alternative gear clusters, or an alternative gearbox altogether (the Ford Escort Twin-Cam, Mexico and RS 1600, for instance, use a stronger gearbox than the other Escorts) may be necessary.

A differential rarely gives trouble unless it runs out of oil. The only problem here is whether the overall gear ratio of the car in standard form is still suitable now that it has been tuned. If the car is being used on the road and for the occasional weekend of motor sport, the chances are that the standard final drive—which on average gives about 16mph, or so, per 1,000 engine rpm in top gear—is a good compromise. On the other hand, if the car is to be fairly seriously used for competition you may need several final drive ratios. On a short circuit, for instance, in club racing it may be an advantage to get to, say, 100mph as quickly as possible, and a final drive ratio should be chosen where 100mph coincides with the maximum safe rpm of the engine.

Half-shafts let you know when they have had enough by breaking—generally when you're in the process of crossing a busy street. As with gearboxes, the only way out of this problem is to fit a stronger component.

Engine Transplants

It is an old adage that from the engineering point of view, very little is impossible. You can, if you want, fit a Buick V8 engine into a Mini—providing you don't mind it driving the front wheels while the engine sits where the back seat normally is. This, in fact, has been done and the car actually went—although it did act a little strangely on the corners.

Engine transplants are not new to the motor manufacturers. The Escort Mexico uses what was originally the Cortina Mk2 GT engine, while the Vauxhall Ventora uses the 3·3 litre engine designed for the Vauxhall Cresta.

On the surface, transplants look easy, but in practice they can become rather complicated. To return to the Escort Mexico for a moment, in addition to the 1600cc engine, the car also has a Corsair 2000E gearbox to take the increased power, and Escort Twin-Cam drive shafts. It has uprated front struts, stiffer rear dampers, radius arms to control the rear axle, wide-rim wheels, radial tyres and a bodyshell reinforced in three areas—at the strut mountings, at the box-sections below the front footwell and at the pick-up points for the radius arms. In fact, it is not so much a transplant as a complete rebuild. So long as you are prepared to accept that a lot of other modifications will be needed to cope with a bigger engine, then a transplant offers a means of owning a highly individual car with a performance that belies its appearance.

I was once slightly involved in a project to fit a 144bhp Ford Zodiac three-litre V6 engine into a 1200cc Mk1 Cortina. A colleague did the conversion himself and the car took about six months to get right. The following is a very telescoped version of what was involved.

The Zodiac engine was mated to a Corsair 2000E gearbox.

The Corsair bell-housing obligingly fits the Zodiac engine, but since the splines on the Corsair first motion shaft are different from the Zodiac, a special clutch disc had to be made up by Automotive Products with the Zodiac overall diameter and the Corsair centre spigot. The reason for choosing the 2000E gearbox was because it fits the Cortina rear mounting. So setting the position of the engine merely involved cutting a hole for the gear lever in the Cortina floor and, with the rear mounting connected, the engine was blocked up on the centre-line of the car and checked for level.

A stronger Corsair V4 front cross-member was then fitted in place of the original and this incorporated the pick-up points for the engine mountings. The mountings had to be specially made and were first shaped from thin sheet tin cut from an old oil can, and the shapes used as templates for marking out the real thing on ⅜in thick mild steel plate, which was then cut, bent and drilled to suit.

With the engine mounted, the next problem was the exhaust manifolding. The standard Zodiac manifolds fouled the steering box, so a new set was made up, using four V4 Corsair manifolds —three left-hand and one right-hand. These were cut and welded to form two six-cylinder manifolds and tucked in closer to the engine without fouling anything. The remainder of the exhaust system incorporated V4 down-pipes joined to a single tail-pipe with a straight-through silencer under the boot floor.

The extra engine capacity required a larger radiator, but since space in front of the unit was limited, a special radiator was made up with the same overall size as the original Cortina one, but with considerably more down-tubes. This was connected to a Zodiac header-tank mounted alongside the engine. The original Zodiac water-pump and fan were discarded because they took up too much room ahead of the engine, and were replaced by a V4 water-pump which fits alongside the front timing gear cover. This meant there was no engine-driven cooling fan, so an electric one was fitted ahead of the radiator, to blow cooling air through it in traffic.

To take the extra weight of the engine, Corsair GT export front springs were fitted in conjunction with up-rated Armstrong front struts. At the rear, stiffer five-leaf springs replaced the standard ones, with up-rated dampers and anti-tramp bars.

The original 1200 Cortina had been fitted with drum brakes. Ideally, these should have been changed to discs at the front, using Lotus-Cortina front struts and the appropriate parts. However, funds were running low by this time and the best alternative was chosen—Ferodo VG 95 anti-fade linings all round, with a Girling 2:1 brake servo. This set-up worked extremely well, giving 82 per cent G at 100lb pedal pressure. Wheels were Dunlop D1 cast aluminium with 5½in rims, shod with Dunlop SP 68 radial tyres.

On its first test the car confirmed that the extra 100bhp or so from the Zodiac engine really made it move. It would accelerate extremely quickly up to 88mph in top, which coincided with the maximum advisable engine rpm of 6,000. In fact, it could reach its maximum speed from a standing start in just about 440 yards. The standing quarter-mile time, incidentally, was 16·2 seconds, and it was recording 0–30mph in 2·8 seconds, 0–60mph in 8·8 seconds and 0–70mph in a fraction over 12 seconds. Top gear acceleration between 20mph and 60mph was better than a 4·2 Jaguar E-type.

But it obviously was not geared properly. The standard 4·1:1 final drive made it all too easy to over-rev, even in top gear, and it did not take long before the inevitable happened and the engine was inadvertently run up to somewhere around 7,500rpm and stripped some of the teeth of the big fibre gearwheel that drives the camshaft. No sooner had this and the appropriate broken rockers and bent pushrods been replaced when there were more teething troubles—this time in the gearbox where the extra punch from the Zodiac engine had chewed a number of teeth off third gear. A little later the teeth on the laygear cluster began to break up.

The gearbox problem was solved by fitting the much stronger gearbox from the Capri 3000 GT. On the face of it this should have been a piece of cake, but it wasn't. The first snag was that it would not fit under the Cortina transmission tunnel like the 2000 gearbox had. So a large section had to be cut away to clear the rod linkage and a suitably shaped piece of mild steel sheet welded over the hole.

The Capri gearbox is developed from the original Zodiac unit, so this meant that the special clutch disc had to be discarded and a standard Capri one used in its place. There was another clutch problem, too. On the old 2000E gearbox the clutch was hydraulically operated by a slave cylinder bolted to the bell-housing. To suit this set-up to the Cortina, all that was changed was the clutch master cylinder, a 2000E cylinder being substituted for the original. On the Capri, the clutch is operated by a cable, but on this the cable would not reach the pedal.

Eventually a compromise was reached. The cable from the clutch was connected to one side of a bell-crank bolted to the side of the engine bay. To the other side of the crank was connected a Mini clutch slave cylinder which was operated by the existing 2000E master cylinder connected to the pedal. The system worked well, but gave a very heavy feel to the pedal, so a brake servo with a ratio of $1\frac{1}{2}$:1 was connected into the hydraulic line and had the desired effect of lightening the pedal load. The only snag now was that with a brake and a clutch servo operating from the same engine inlet manifold, there were times when there was not sufficient vacuum to go round, so a vacuum storage tank was added (from an Austin A/110) to provide a reserve supply for both servos.

This was not the end of the gearbox difficulties, for the bulkier Capri box would not fit the original rear mounting, so the underside of the bodyshell had to be modified (by the addition of a large piece of angle-iron) to accept the Capri rear mounting. The prop-shaft was too long as well, and the front mounting splines did not mate up with those on the Capri gearbox. This problem was solved by sending the shaft to a specialist, stating the length required and specifying a Capri 3000 coupling at one end and a Cortina 1200 the other. I often wonder what he thought . . .

To get the revs down, the 4·1 final drive was taken out and replaced by one with a ratio of 3·55:1. Unfortunately, the Capri 3000 ratio of 3·24 would not fit or this would have been used. With the Capri gearbox and revised overall gearing, the maximum speed improved to 115mph, although the acceleration times suffered a little. The 0–30mph time was now 3 sec, with 0–60mph in 9 sec, 0–70mph in 12·2 sec, and—for the first time—a 0–90mph time of 21·2 sec. The standing quarter went up 0·7 sec to 16·9 sec.

If the above account discourages you, then it is probably better that you are put off now, rather than half-way through a transplant job when you have spent a fair amount of money. For those who are not put off, it should be said, in fairness, that there are easier transplant operations than this. For instance, the V4 engine is much easier to fit into the Cortina than the V6, while on earlier cars it is possible to switch the 1500 and 1200 Cortina engine into the Anglia 105E without even changing the engine mountings. The same applies to substituting a 1600 crossflow for a 1300.

With British Leyland vehicles, it is a straightforward job to put, say, an 1100 engine into a Mini. The external dimensions are the same, although the engine mounting on the radiator side must be changed for an 1100 one. It is also important to realise that the 1100 uses a final drive ratio of 4·1:1 and the 850 Mini has a 3·7 final drive, so this should be changed before the 1100 engine is slipped in.

Typical Results

The following figures show the sort of improvement against the stop-watch that various stages of tune can give. To put the figures in perspective, a small saloon car that covers 0–60mph in less than 14 seconds and a sports car that does the same in less than 11 seconds, are reckoned to be pretty lively. Standard performances, unless otherwise indicated, are in brackets.

CORTINA MK2 1600 GT
Modification: Allard-Shorrock
C 142B supercharger. Maximum boost
7psi, one 2in SU carburettor

mph	sec	
0–30	4·0	(4·1)
0–40	5·6	(6·1)
0–50	7·7	(9·1)
0–60	10·2	(13·1)
0–70	13·9	(17·8)
0–80	18·0	(26·6)

Maximum speed: 110mph (100mph)
Fuel consumption: (overall) 21mpg (25mpg)

TRIUMPH 2000
SAH Stage 4 Engine conversion comprising: 10·5:1 compression ratio
cylinder head with enlarged inlet ports, larger inlet valves and stiffer valve
springs; modified camshaft, six-branch exhaust manifold, dual-silencer
exhaust system; three twin-choke Weber 40 DCOE carburettors, sports
ignition coil, oil cooler.

mph	sec	
0– 30	3·6	(4·0)
0– 40	5·0	(6·5)
0– 50	6·1	(8·9)
0– 60	9·0	(12·8)
0– 70	11·9	(17·5)
0– 80	15·0	(23·0)
0– 90	19·2	—
0–100	25·7	—

Maximum speed: 124mph (95·1mph)
Fuel consumption: (overall) 20mpg (24mpg)

HILLMAN IMP
The acceleration with four stages of Hartwell tuning are compared here.
(A) has twin 1½in Stromberg CD carburettors on a special inlet manifold
(B) the above plus a four-branch exhaust manifold and straight-through
   silencer
(C) includes A and B plus a Hartwell high-torque camshaft. The final
   stage
(D) includes all the above plus increasing the engine capacity to 998cc by
   boring out, fitting wet liners and larger diameter pistons. In addition
   the cylinder head is modified, with bigger inlet valves and stiffer valve
   springs.

Standard		(A) Twin carburettors	(B) + exhaust	(C) + camshaft	(D) 998cc
mph	sec	sec	sec	sec	sec
0–40	8·1	7·8	7·1	6·7	5·9
0–50	13·0	12·1	11·0	10·0	8·6
0–60	19·7	17·0	15·5	14·5	11·7
0–70	32·5	27·2	21·7	20·1	16·8

FORD ESCORT GT
Ford Stage 2 improved performance kit fitted comprising modified Weber
32 DFM progressive twin-choke down-draught carburettor, reworked
inlet manifold, modified cylinder head with improved porting and compression ratio raised by 0·4 to 9·6:1. Improved four-branch exhaust
system. Note the fuel consumption after conversion.

mph	sec	
0–50	7·1	(8·8)
0–60	9·8	(12·5)
0–70	13·8	(17·4)
0–80	18·5	(25·9)
0–90	24·0	(41·2)
Top gear		
20–40	9·8	(10·6)
40–60	9·8	(10·2)

Maximum speed: 106·5mph (93·4mph)
Fuel consumption: (overall) 26·2mpg (25·3mpg)

AUSTIN MINI
Oselli big-bore engine conversion, enlarging the capacity from 848cc to
1125cc by boring and fitting longer-throw crankshaft, new con-rods and
pistons and heavy-duty crankshaft bearings. Cylinder head modified to
give 10:1 compression ratio, standard-size valves with stiffer springs, twin
1¼in SU carburettors, three-branch exhaust manifold, straight-through
silencer. Standard figures are for a typical 848cc Mini.

mph	sec	
0–30	4·0	(6·0)
0–40	6·2	(9·9)
0–50	10·5	(17·6)
0–60	14·2	(28·3)
0–70	21·4	—

Maximum speed: 89·9mph (72mph)

ESCORT 1600
Modified by Race-Proved who removed the standard engine and fitted the
Cortina 1600 GT engine in its place. In this instance the conversion was
carried out on an Escort Estate car; the standard figures are those for an
Escort 1300 Saloon.

mph	sec	
0–30	3·8	(4·5)
0–40	5·9	(7·1)
0–50	8·5	(11·8)
0–60	12·4	(16·2)
0–70	17·0	(24·2)
0–80	26·0	—

Fuel consumption: (overall) 32mpg (36mpg)

AUSTIN MAXI 1500
This was a prototype British Leyland Special Tuning conversion for road

use. Twin 1¼in SUs are fitted with a four-branch exhaust manifold, a bigger-bore exhaust system and a straight-through silencer. This particular car was also fitted with light-weight Minilite Magnesium road wheels and light-weight glass-fibre side and back doors and a glass-fibre bonnet.

mph	sec	
0–30	3·5	(4·9)
0–40	5·9	(8·3)
0–50	8·4	(11·6)
0–60	12·2	(17·4)
0–70	17·4	(24·5)
0–80	25·4	—

Maximum speed: 101mph (5th), 90·8mph (4th)

VAUXHALL VIVA 1600 OHC
Car fitted with Coburn carburettor kit comprising a Nikki dual choke 32/35 carburettor fitted to the standard inlet manifold using an adaptor plate.

mph	sec	
0–60	13·7	(18)

Maximum speed: 98mph (86mph)
Fuel consumption: (overall) 34·1mpg (24mpg)

6
PERFORMANCE EXTRAS

The number of performance extras your car needs depends on how many it was provided with in the first place. Cars like the Jaguar E-Type, or the Triumph Stag, come well equipped with instruments, powerful headlamps, an alternator to maintain the battery in an adequate state of charge, and comfortable seats that give an ideal driving position. But if you have modified a relatively humble family saloon to go faster, the standard equipment may not cope so well with its extra potential. Fortunately, matters can be improved either by altering the existing equipment or by adding a selection of the bolt-on extras available from accessory shops.

Speedometer Every road-going car has a speedometer, but few are really accurate, most giving slightly optimistic readings, particularly at higher speeds. If you live near a motorway, the accuracy of the speedometer can be checked using the marker posts in the centre or on the side of the road. Depending on the stretch you use, the posts are 55 or 110 yards apart—four or eight intervals add up to a quarter-mile.

To calibrate the speedometer you need a helper with a stop-

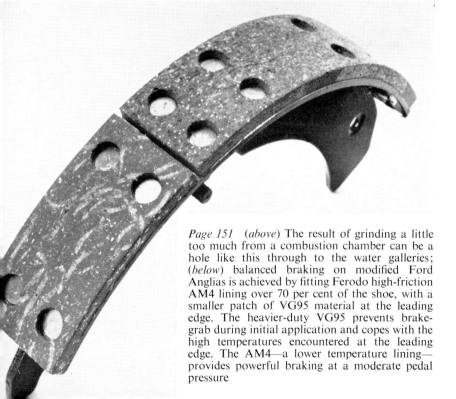

Page 151 (*above*) The result of grinding a little
too much from a combustion chamber can be a
hole like this through to the water galleries;
(*below*) balanced braking on modified Ford
Anglias is achieved by fitting Ferodo high-friction
AM4 lining over 70 per cent of the shoe, with a
smaller patch of VG95 material at the leading
edge. The heavier-duty VG95 prevents brake-
grab during initial application and copes with the
high temperatures encountered at the leading
edge. The AM4—a lower temperature lining—
provides powerful braking at a moderate pedal
pressure

Page 152 (*above left*) Cutting an oblong hole in a bonnet-top using a Monodex nibbler; (*above*) into a hole goes a louvre panel, here being blended with the surrounding metal using plastic filler; (*below left*) the finished job. A stage-by-stage description is given in Chapter 8

watch. Pick a time when the motorway is not busy and drive at a steady 30, 40, 50, 60 and 70mph while your helper times the car at each speed over a quarter-mile. If you are not sure of the intervals between the posts, these can be roughly checked if you remember that at a steady 30mph, the car travels 440 yards in 30 seconds, and at 60mph, 15 seconds.

Novices with the stop-watch sometimes make the mistake of counting the first post—when the watch is started—as number one. Where posts are at 110yd intervals, the watch is started as the car passes a post and the *next* post is counted as no 1, and the watch is stopped as the car passes post no 4, like this:

post		post		post		post		post
—	110yd	—	110yd	—	110yd	—	110yd	—
Start		1		2		3		4
watch								Stop
								watch

In fact, counting the post where the watch is started, five posts are involved; working on the same principle, nine posts at 55yd intervals are used. The time taken in seconds for the car to cover the flying quarter-mile is divided into 900 and the result is the true speed in mph.

We have already seen that at 60mph the quarter-mile should be covered in 15 seconds. Let us assume that at 60mph on the speedometer, your car in fact covers the distance in 16 seconds. This gives a true speed of $\frac{900}{16} = 56.25$mph which shows the speedometer to be 3.75mph fast.

Although not accurate in a scientific sense, the quick way to calibrate the speedometer at this point would be to regard an indicated 63.75mph as a true 60mph. In practice, after allowing for speedometer needle waver, you would call this 64mph. The same calculation is made at other speeds and you will end up with a series of corrected readings. The sort of error you can expect is something like this:

K

True	30	40	50	60	70	mph
Indicated	32	42	53	64	75	

Unfortunately, there is nothing you can adjust on the instrument to improve its accuracy, and the normal method of correction is to mark the speedometer glass with a wax pencil or stick on small paper arrows to show the true speeds. You will then be able to take accurate before-and-after acceleration times.

Besides a speedometer, most small cars have a fuel gauge and for some this is the total instrumentation provided, warning lights being fitted to indicate low oil pressure, lack of dynamo charge and perhaps high water temperature. Warning lights are far better than nothing and are more likely to be noticed by the average motorist. But they have the disadvantage that they only come on when most of the damage has been done. Take an oil-pressure light, for instance. The switch is designed to operate when the oil pressure has dropped to 4–7psi. On an engine that may be turning at 4,000rpm and normally operates at 60psi a drop of 53psi or more in oil pressure would at least damage the crankshaft bearings—maybe scoring the crankshaft itself. An oil-pressure gauge, on the other hand, will warn of a gradual drop in pressure and if an unaccustomed 10psi is lost there is time to stop and investigate before any damage is caused.

Oil-pressure Gauge On engines with an oil-pressure warning light it is possible to use the same take-off point for the gauge. In fact, as a 'belt-and-braces' measure it is customary to screw a Tee-piece into the block, taking the oil-pressure warning light off one end and the gauge off the other. Most bolt-on pressure gauges use a copper pipe between the instrument and the pick-up point. The gauge can be detached from the pipe for ease of fitting, and the only point to watch is that the pipe should have two or three coils put in it between the mounting on the engine and the first point where it is clipped to the body/chassis. These coils will absorb the movement of the engine.

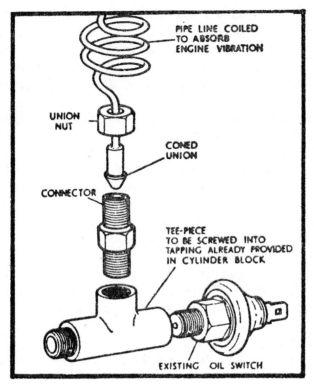

PIPE LINE COILED
TO ABSORB
ENGINE VIBRATION

UNION
NUT

CONED
UNION

CONNECTOR

TEE-PIECE
TO BE SCREWED INTO
TAPPING ALREADY PROVIDED
IN CYLINDER BLOCK

EXISTING OIL SWITCH

FIG 48

An oil-pressure gauge Tee-piece connection allows the
fitting of the gauge and the existing warning light

Water-temperature Gauge These gauges are available in two
varieties—electrical and capillary. The capillary type is generally
the more accurate and uses the thermometer method to move
the needle. Broadly speaking, a sensor filled with volatile fluid
(ether) is plumbed into the cooling system, the sensor being connected to the instrument by a small-bore tube. The ether
expands as the engine heats up and the expansion begins to
uncurl a bent piece of tube—known as a Bourdon tube—inside
the instrument. The Bourdon tube is connected to the needle
which gives the appropriate reading.

The sensor is usually mounted in a tapped hole provided by the car manufacturer near the thermostat area, or alternatively it may be fitted into the top radiator hose, or the radiator header tank. Sensors on the radiator side of the thermostat will only show a reading on the gauge after the thermostat has opened.

Electrical water-temperature gauges work on the variable resistance method. Instead of a sensor, a transmitter is used at the engine end. Heating it varies its resistance and this is detected by the instrument. The advantage of electrical gauges is that they only require one cable connection between the transmitter and gauge. Capillary-type gauges cannot be detached from the small-bore tube, so a large hole must be made in the bulkhead to get the sensor and its locking screw through. Electrical gauges can give false readings if a connection is bad and they are of the quadrant-type where the needle moves through an arc of less than 90 degrees, whereas a capillary gauge can have a more accurate full-scale dial like a speedometer.

Vacuum Gauge Sometimes referred to as a 'performance gauge', this is connected to the engine inlet manifold by a tube and measures the depression within the manifold in inches of mercury (in Hg). Most production-line engines idle at 17–21in Hg and naturally this reading drops when the throttle is opened and a petrol/air mixture at atmospheric pressure rushes into the manifold. When driving on a level road at a light throttle opening, a standard engine in good condition should record 10–16in Hg. Keeping the vacuum reading as high as possible will result in the engine giving its best fuel consumption.

The vacuum gauge is a very active instrument, the needle responding to the tiniest movement of the accelerator, and its sensitivity is claimed to be helpful in tracking down internal engine faults ranging from worn piston rings, sticking valves and gasket failure to incorrectly set ignition timing. Most gauges come with a diagnostic chart which tells you what any odd readings mean.

For modified engines, which should already be in good condition, the principal use of the vacuum gauge is for tuning a carburettor. It is essential for tuning a Fish carburettor accurately (see Chapter 7) and is useful when adjusting SU or Stromberg CD carburettors, when the method used is to set the idling speed to around 2,000rpm and adjust the mixture to give the highest vacuum reading. Incidentally, on engines which have been modified by fitting a wide overlap camshaft, the vacuum reading at tick-over speed will be less than the 17–21in Hg quoted for a standard engine. This is because the overlap allows some blow-back into the inlet manifold at tick-over speeds.

When fitting the gauge the entry point into the manifold should be made downstream of the throttle butterfly (do not use the take-off pipe for the distributor vacuum unit) and it is preferable if the hole is drilled in the top of the manifold since this will prevent petrol from getting into the vacuum line. If possible, use a removable plug as a mounting point for the line connector, but make sure that the plug leads into the manifold and not the water jacket that surrounds some inlet manifolds.

It is unlikely, but possible, that the vacuum connector will simply replace the plug. But if it will not, remove the plug, drill it, tap it to accept the connector and re-fit it. On cars without a spare manifold plug, but which have closed-circuit crankcase breathing systems, the large union which connects the breather hose to the manifold can be removed and a hole drilled in the side of the union—on one of the hexagon flats—to accept the connector. Where the manifold itself is to be drilled and tapped, it must be removed from the engine in order to clean out any metal particles which drop inside. Some mechanics may argue that greasing the drill and tap will hold the metal filings, but against this must be weighed the fact that one fragment of metal trapped under a valve means that the cylinder head must come off to grind in all the valves.

On cars with more than one carburettor, a vacuum gauge can either be fitted in the balance pipe between two carburettors, or

one instrument can be used on each carburettor. For cost
reasons, multiple vacuum gauges are rarely fitted, although for
tuning purposes it should be possible to provide one vacuum
gauge connection per carburettor, each connection normally
being kept closed, and only being opened-up for tuning with a
gauge.

Tachometer This indicates engine speed in revolutions per
minute and is essential where the valve gear has been modified
to allow the engine to reach higher-than-normal rpm. It has

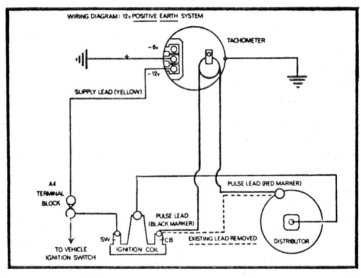

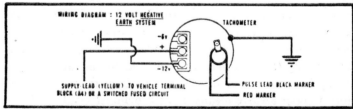

FIG 49

Typical wiring diagram for an impulse-type tachometer. Note reversal of
connections for positive- or negative-earth polarity

already been noted that most production-line engines are self-governing because valve float or the limitations of the carburettor or inlet manifold make them 'run out of breath' before they can be over-revved to the point where damage may be caused. But if these limitations are removed, the inertia and centrifugal force of the moving parts increase in proportion to the square of the engine speed. This means that increasing engine speed by 20 per cent—say from 5,000rpm to 6,000rpm—will put 44 per cent greater stress on the moving parts.

Most tachometers are of the impulse type and work electronically by sensing pulses in the low-tension ignition circuit. They are available in 6v or 12v applications, for engines with 4, 6 or 8 cylinders and calibrated 0–8,000rpm or 0–10,000rpm—so there is plenty to think about when choosing one. Most are adaptable for positive or negative earth and, since the instrument uses transistors which burn out if current is passed through them from the wrong direction, it is important to check the car's polarity before wiring-up.

Electric Fan As a rule, water-cooled engines use a belt-driven fan to draw or push air through the radiator core. Estimates on how much engine power is wasted in turning this fan vary from 3bhp to 25bhp depending on the engine and who you listen to. But there is no doubt that the cooling fan absorbs *some* power, and it is also true that on cars with front-mounted radiators the fan is unnecessary at speeds above about 25mph because the natural airflow takes over. In fact, if your journeys do not involve traffic jams or very slow motoring, there is no reason why the fan-blades should not be removed—at least in the winter.

Cars with side or rear-mounted radiators and vehicles that endure the occasional traffic snarl-up need some artificial means of pushing air through the radiator core, and the best alternative to the power-robbing belt-driven fan is a thermostatically-controlled electric one.

Electric fans are available as bolt-on kits to suit most vehicles, the more popular units using a very flat electric motor that gives a total depth, including the fan-blade, of just over 3in, which allows fitting to almost any vehicle. On transverse-engined cars, where space is particularly limited, the fan is fitted in the wheel arch.

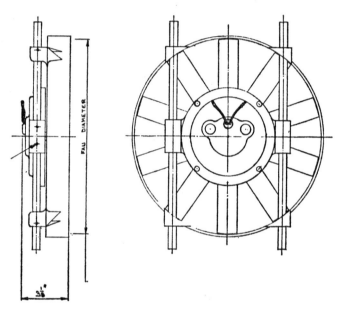

FIG 50

Wood-Jeffreys electric cooling fan with 'flat' type motor

Both the principal manufacturers of these units—Kenlowe and Wood-Jeffreys—provide a thermostatic control which can be set to cut in the fan when the engine water temperature reaches a pre-determined level—on most engines a suitable cut-in point is around 83–87°C. A temperature gauge is, of course, essential.

A cheaper way of installing an electric fan is to use an old heater blower motor and connect to it one of the more efficient moulded plastic fans, such as one from a Ford Escort.

Before embarking on a 'do-it-yourself' electric fan project some advance planning is advisable. The main point to watch is that a motor with the correct direction of rotation is purchased, since a number of heater motors will not reverse direction simply by swapping the connections to the battery. But before you can decide the direction of rotation, you must know on which side of the radiator the motor will be fitted, and the correct direction of rotation of the fan (turning a fan back-to-front will *not* change a 'blower' into a 'sucker'). With this information you should be able to pick a suitable motor. If you want to save the cost of a thermal switch, the 'do-it-yourself' fan can be manually switched, preferably using a switch with a warning light which indicates when the fan is in use. You will, of course, need to keep an eye on the temperature gauge.

Variable-pitch Fans These replace the standard fan blades and, therefore, are still turned by the fan belt. However, much of the effort that the fan belt wastes in turning the fan at high engine speeds is saved because the blades feather.

There are two basic types. On one the blades are spring-loaded so that they adopt a fairly coarse pitch when the engine is turning slowly, but as the revs build up, air pressure on the blades causes them to 'bend in the wind', so to speak, and feather to a finer pitch. The only drawback with this device comes when the car is being worked hard in the lower gears, such as when climbing a long, steep hill. Then the high engine speeds will feather the fan, but at the same time the air flow may not be sufficient to cool the radiator and the engine may overheat.

An alternative method of feathering the blades is to use a temperature-sensitive 'clock-spring' to operate the blades. Increased temperature expands the spring and puts the blades on to a coarse pitch. As the temperature drops, the spring contracts, feathering the fan. This unit gets over the problem of the long hill, low speeds and high engine revs.

Oil Cooler As engine oil heats up it loses viscoscity or, if you like, becomes thinner, and this has the effect of lowering the oil pressure and increasing the risk of bearing damage. In addition, if oil is seriously overheated some of its constituents begin to fractionate off and the quality of the oil deteriorates.

A few performance cars are fitted with oil coolers as standard equipment, but most saloon cars, Volkswagen excepted, do not have one, mainly because in standard form they are unlikely to overheat the oil. But if the engine has been modified it may need a cooler. For high oil temperature is caused mainly by high engine revolutions, and most modified engines rev higher than standard.

An oil-cooler layout is similar to a water-cooling system. A small radiator is placed in the airstream and oil piped through it. Most coolers pick up their oil supply at the oil filter. There are three methods of doing this. A sandwich plate containing an intake and outlet pipe may be fitted between the oil filter bowl and its housing; alternatively, on engines which have a

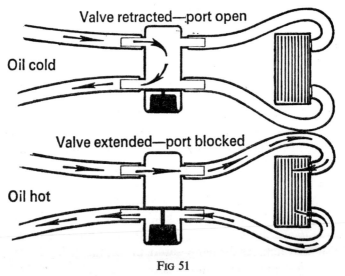

FIG 51

Thermostatic control on an oil-cooler circuit

screw-in, throw-away filter canister, an adaptor may be provided which goes around the hollow fixing bolt. On engines with external oil pipes, like the BLMC 'A' and 'B' Series units, the pipe is removed and the oil cooler linked up in its place.

Some oil coolers incorporate a thermostat which prevents the oil being passed through the radiator until the oil temperature has reached 80°C. It is not generally realised that cold oil, besides causing an unnecessary drag on the crankshaft, also causes engine damage over a period. At low temperatures, oil absorbs the water which always forms inside the crankcase as condensation each time the engine cools. Ideally, this water is liberated as the oil heats up. But if an efficient oil cooler keeps the oil temperature well below 80°C, the water is retained and combines with other impurities to form sludge. At excessively low temperatures, some of the combustion gases which blow past the piston rings can combine with the water and form sulphuric acid which will attack bearing surfaces. An oil-cooler thermostat costs between £3 and £4 and in my view is worth the money. The alternative is to blank off the oil-cooler radiator

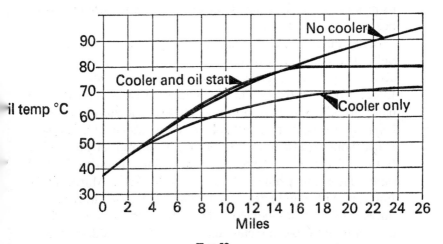

Fig 52

Oil-temperature graphs on an 1800cc car over the same route

during the winter, which can be inconvenient if the cooler is placed behind the grille. To control the maximum temperature the oil will reach, the size of the radiator is altered. It is not always obvious whether or not a car needs an oil cooler. The best way to find out is to motor at the legal maximum along a motorway for at least fifteen miles and watch the oil-pressure gauge. If the pressure drops steadily below the normal hot reading as the distance increases, assuming the engine is in reasonable condition, it could benefit from an oil cooler which will maintain the oil pressure at the normal maximum.

Improved Lighting The headlamps on most British cars are fitted with two tungsten filaments, a 45 watt one for dip beam and a 60 watt filament for high beam. The high-beam filament is rated at about 45,000 candlepower.

It is possible to improve on this in a number of ways, the easiest being to replace the 7in diameter standard Lucas 60/45 sealed-beam light units with identical-looking tungsten filament light units, also from Lucas, but with a 75 watt (52,000cp) high-beam filament and a 50 watt dip. This unit has been designed to produce a much whiter light on high beam without loss of beam control. They cost about £4 a pair.

Better than tungsten lighting is a lamp fitted with a halogen bulb. The bulbs are expensive, but for the same voltage give about 30 per cent increase in light over a conventional bulb. Lucas makes 7in light units which accept a twin-filament 60/50 halogen bulb. The bulb produces 60,000 candlepower on high beam, and a pair of these light units cost about £11. Halogen conversions are also available for four-headlamp cars, both high beam and dip lamps being fitted with single filament 55 watt bulbs. These are a standard fitment to the Aston Martin DBS. For cars with non-sealed rectangular headlamps, Mazda produces a 60/55 twin-filament halogen bulb conversion, and for cars with sealed-beam rectangular lamps, Cibié produces a conversion with a twin-filament halogen bulb.

Comfort If every driver was 5ft 6in tall and had the same arm length, leg length and shoe size, all cars would be comfortable. Unfortunately, all production cars of the same model are the same size, but the drivers who use them are not. Within limitations of price, the manufacturers do what they can to provide reasonably shaped seats with a moderate amount of adjustment. But they cannot please everyone, and it is hardly surprising that some people find certain cars uncomfortable after the first 150 miles.

If you are uncomfortable in a car, the chances are that you will drive badly—even if only to get home and sit in a comfortable chair. Fortunately, even the worst car can be improved, maybe by modifying the seat and the position of some controls. The ideal driving position is one from where you can see where you are going without any neck craning (remember seats compress with age) and with the whole of your back supported by the seat back. From this position you should be able to grip the top of the steering wheel rim lightly with both hands with your arms almost straight and it should be possible to press all pedals to the floor without twisting in the seat. The gear lever should be in easy reach, and preferably the seat will have some side support to brace you on sharp corners.

If repositioning or blocking up the standard seat will not improve the driving position, a number of optional seats are available from accessory shops, all of which have the virtue of looking extremely comfortable in the shop. Before buying one, sit in it in the shop (some bucket seats are very narrow) and if it fits your shape, make sure it has all the appropriate runners to suit it to your car.

On some cars like the Mini and Hillman Imp it is possible to lower the height of the steering wheel. This involves slackening off the mountings on the steering rack, undoing the steering column clamp, inserting a spacer between the clamp and the column to alter the rake of the column, and tightening everything up. Once you have found the right spanners, on a Mini the job takes about ten minutes.

It is worth mentioning that BLMC do not approve of this modification, although it is a popular one on private competition Minis and a great number of road cars. Possibly one of the reasons for works' disapproval is the fact that it is possible to fit the lowering spacer without loosening the rack. This obviously puts a great strain on the pinion shaft at the toe-board, and this shaft has been known to break when this is done, leaving the car without any steering. Some steering-column-lowering kits have been sold without any fitting instructions, which suggests to the uninitiated, perhaps, that very little dismantling is needed. But whenever fitting a lowering device, the rack *must* be loosened and re-tightened afterwards.

Small lightweight steering wheels have been a popular bolt-on extra for a number of years. Besides looking attractive, a lightweight wheel really does give a more positive feel to the steering, and if it is smaller in diameter than the standard one, there is less arm-twirling required to get round a tight corner, although the steering will be a little heavier. It is possible to obtain special wheels with a substantially dished centre, which puts the rim a little closer to the driver—a point worth remembering where you are considering moving the seat further back.

Once the seating and the position of the steering wheel have been improved, you have a wide choice of discretionary extras which apply to most cars and which may or may not improve the comfort of your particular vehicle. Under this heading come self-evident items like switch extensions, gear lever extensions and electric windscreen washer conversions, while some cars— again, the Mini is the most likely—benefit from having a centrally-mounted instrument transferred to a position ahead of the driver where it can be seen more easily. On the Mini this is a straightforward but fiddly job, involving lengthening all the wiring connections to the speedometer head, and the use of the longer speedometer cable from a BLMC 1100 or 1300.

Alternators On a rainy night, a car using two 75 watt head-lamps, plus a couple of 60 watt auxiliary lamps in addition to its windscreen wipers and heater blower motor, will be draining about 30 amps from its battery. The average small-car dynamo has a maximum output of 22–25 amps, so, with this load, the battery begins to lose its charge and will gradually go flat unless the load is reduced to below the maximum dynamo output.

On cars with a large number of electrical accessories the way to avoid a slowly flattening battery is to replace the dynamo with an alternator. Alternators produce a bigger output over a wider rev-range than a dynamo, and to keep an alternator turning fairly quickly, it is normally geared up about 2:1 in relation to engine speed. Lucas quotes 15,000rpm as the maxi-

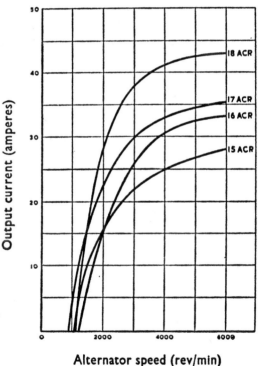

Alternator speed (rev/min)

Fig 53

Typical Lucas alternator outputs

mum speed of its most popular replacement alternators. By comparison, a dynamo is likely to be geared down in relation to engine speed. Most production dynamos have a maximum speed of 4,000rpm and produce their peak output from around 2,000rpm. Below 1,400rpm they may not produce anything at all.

The Lucas 17 ACR alternator, which is a popular dynamo replacement, delivers 22 amps at 2,000rpm. Assuming it is geared up 2:1, this output is available at 1,000 engine rpm—tickover speed on the majority of modified engines. The 17 ACR's maximum output of 36 amps is available from 6,000 alternator rpm—3,000rpm of the engine. A 43 amp alternator is also available. These alternators are reasonably straightforward to fit, but only suit 12 volt negative-earth systems. Cars wired 12 volt positive earth can have the polarity changed to accept an alternator.

7
TUNING AND TESTING

Most people know that the carburettor's main function is to mix petrol with the air going into the engine. Preferably, the ratio of air to petrol by weight should be around 13:1 for normal running, slightly richer when accelerating, and a good deal richer—perhaps as high as 4:1—for cold starting.

Bearing in mind that carburettors have been with us for almost as long as the car itself, it is a little surprising that no one has perfected a way of accurately calculating in advance the correct carburettor setting for a particular engine. What happens when a new engine is designed is that the carburettor manufacturers calculate the *approximate* jets and/or needles—and then they put the engine on a test-bed to see if they were right. Quite often they are nearly right, but a continual process of trial-and-error on the test-bed is required before they eventually arrive at the final settings.

The way the correct setting for an SU is found, for instance, is to fit a test needle of what the engineers think is the right taper, and then run the engine at various speeds and loads. Let us assume that the engine is loaded until it operates at full throttle at 2,000, 3,000, 4,000 and 5,000rpm. At each loading the piston lift is accurately measured. Then the jet in which the needle works is raised or lowered until the engine produces its maximum power with the weakest mixture. Because the engineers know the taper of the test needle, the amount of piston lift and the exact position of the jet, they can calculate the ideal needle diameter for each engine load. The same sort of 'suck-it-and-see' testing is carried out on fixed-choke carburettors, but with these a certain amount of inspired guesswork, coupled with hard experience, is needed to decide which jets to adjust at which engine speeds. Since these all inter-act, it can be a very complicated business.

Unfortunately, not many of us have access to an engine dynamometer or an exhaust-gas analyser, so that when it comes to the jetting or needling of a carburettor we are at the mercy of the experts to some extent. Fortunately, it is not difficult to obtain information on recommended needles for SU and Stromberg CD carburettors, since the manufacturers publish booklets listing them. A number of these are given in a table at the end of this chapter.

Fixed-choke carburettors are somewhat different. Most tuning shops which produce Weber carburettor kits keep their jet and choke settings a closely guarded secret, and the only way to find out is to buy a kit, take the carburettor to pieces, measure the choke diameters and note down the sizes of all the jets. If you have a fixed-choke carburettor given to you, you can get some idea of the appropriate jetting if you know the jet sizes used on a similar capacity engine. These settings can be used as a starting-point, and to this end I have included the jetting and choke sizes for the twin-choke Weber carburettors fitted to the Escort 1300 GT in various stages of tune.

SU Carburettors

The bulk of British Leyland cars use these carburettors, and the most popular on small cars is the HS type, which is dis-

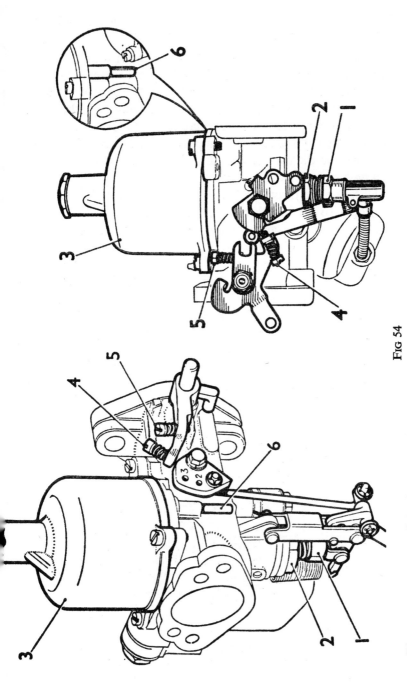

Fig 54

The two most common SUs, the HS (*right*) and H type, showing (1) the jet adjusting nut; (2) jet locking nut; (3) piston suction chamber; (4) fast idle screw; (5) throttle stop screw; (6) piston lifting pin

tinguished by the flexible petrol pipe that connects the bottom of the float chamber to the jet assembly. The earlier version of this unit, the H type, has a slightly different jet assembly, choke linkage and float valve, but the method of tuning it is the same.

When tuning a single SU carburettor, the first essential is to get the engine up to running temperature and then switch it off. Remove the air cleaner and disconnect the choke cable. The tuning sequence is then as follows:

Unscrew the throttle adjusting screw until it is just clear of its stop with the throttle closed. Now set it $1\frac{1}{4}$ turns open. Mark the piston/suction chamber unit to ensure correct reassembly, undo the two fixing screws and lift the chamber and piston off.

Now screw up the jet adjusting nut until the jet is flush with the carburettor bridge, or as far up as it will go. Refit the piston/suction chamber as marked and check, using the piston lifting-pin, that the piston falls freely on to the carburettor bridge when the pin is released. If it does not, see 'jet centring' a little further on.

Unscrew the jet adjusting nut two complete turns, restart the engine and rotate the throttle adjusting screw to give the

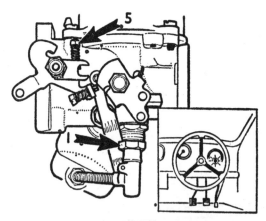

Fig 55

Turn the jet adjusting nut and throttle adjusting screw until the smoothest idling speed is obtained

desired engine idling speed (usually about 500–800rpm, indicated when the ignition warning light just glows).

Turn the jet adjusting nut up to weaken or down to richen the mixture and listen to the idling note. The correct mixture is indicated when the fastest and smoothest idling speed is obtained.

Re-set the throttle adjusting screw to give the appropriate idling speed if necessary, then re-check the mixture strength, using the piston lifting-pin. Raise the piston a *very small* amount, about ¹⁄₃₂in, and note the effect on engine rpm. As can be seen from the graph, the engine will speed up if the mixture is too rich and will stall if it is too weak, whereas correct mixture is indicated if the revs rise slightly, then fall back to somewhere near the original idling speed. It is easy to muff this check because there is a tendency for most people to lift the piston too much, which causes the engine to stall regardless of mixture strength. The only way to get the amount of lift right is to do the job very slowly, gently lifting the pin until you feel it has taken up all the free play and is just contacting the piston. You then need a steady hand to raise it just a fraction more.

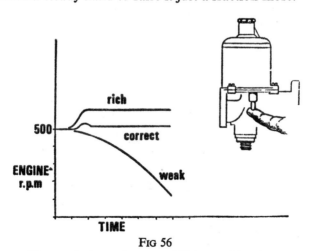

Fig 56

The graph shows three possibilities resulting from
raising the piston ¹⁄₃₂in

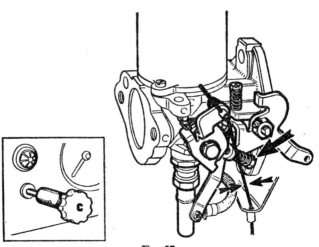

FIG 57

Choke linkage fast-idle adjustment

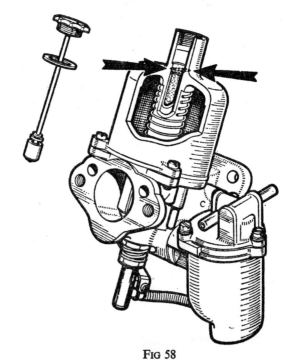

FIG 58

On all except dustproofed carburettors (see text) the piston
rod should be topped up to this level with SAE 20 oil

The next stage is to reconnect the choke control cable, allowing about ₁₆in free movement at the choke knob before it starts to pull on the jet lever. Now pull the choke knob out until the linkage is just about to move the carburettor jet and adjust the fast-idle screw on the choke linkage to give an engine speed of about 1,000rpm (ignition warning light out) when hot.

Lastly, top up the piston damper with the recommended engine oil—SAE 20—until the level is ½in above the top of the hollow piston rod. On dust-proofed carburettors—these have no vent hole in the damper cap and a transverse drilling in the neck of the suction chamber—the oil level should be ½in below the top of the hollow piston rod.

Multiple SUs

As before, warm up the engine, disconnect the choke cable, set the throttle adjusting screws then slacken the clamping bolts or a single clamp (see H type, later on) on the throttle spindle linkage. Now check that the piston drops freely on to the jet

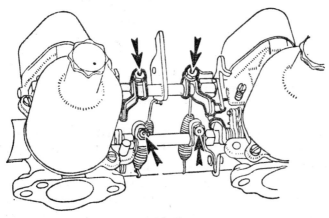

Fig 59

Typical multiple HS type throttle and choke linkage showing linkage adjusting points bridge, as detailed in the single carburettor section, and undo each carburettor jet adjusting nut two complete turns.

You now need a short length of flexible tube—a piece of ⅜in bore pvc is ideal—to use as a stethoscope. Restart the engine and adjust the idling speed with the throttle adjusting screws to about 500rpm, then use the tube to listen to the intake hiss at the mouth of each carburettor. Alter the adjusting screws until the intake hiss from each carburettor is the same. A point worth

Fig 60

Comparing throttle opening on twin SUs by listening to the intake hiss

watching during this operation is that the end of the tube is placed in the same position on each carburettor, since the intake noise gets louder closer to the piston.

With the throttle opening set, turn the jet adjusting nuts on all carburettors a little at a time, up to weaken or down to richen the mixture, until the fastest idling speed is obtained. Now check the mixture strength as before, using the piston lifting-pin on each carburettor. The indications of a rich or weak mixture are the same as with the single carburettor. Alter the jet adjusting nut on the carburettor being tested, then repeat the operation on the other carburettors. Since all carburettors are inter-dependent, re-check until all of them indicate the correct mixture strength. The exhaust pipe gives a clue as to whether the mixture strength is right. With the engine ticking-over, a 'splashy' irregular note, with the occasional misfire and a colourless exhaust, indicates the mixture is too weak. If the mixture is too

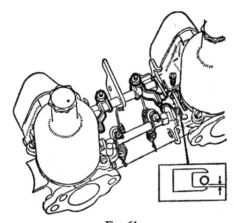

Fig 61

A fork-and-pin arrangement is used on multiple HS carburettor linkages. The gap indicated should be ·006in

rich, the exhaust has a rhythmical misfire, possibly with a trace of black smoke. Correct mixture is indicated by a regular and even exhaust beat, and no smoke.

Once the carburettors have been balanced and set, the linkage is coupled up. There is a slight variation of procedure here, depending on whether HS or H type carburettors are fitted. *On HS types* there is a fork and pin arrangement (see diagram) which allows some play in the linkage. This is set with a feeler gauge so that the link pin is ·006in away from the lower edge of the fork, after which the clamp bolts are tightened. *On H type carburettors*, there is a slightly different linkage system, and it is only necessary to slacken one clamp bolt to separate each pair of carburettors. When re-coupling these, the single clamp is tightened, then a link pin and lever are adjusted as shown in the H type diagram. This provides a slight delay in opening the front carburettor throttle. It is normally only fitted where large multiple layouts are used, and the slightly progressive action cuts down the effort needed to move the butterflies against the drag of the manifold vacuum at tick-over speeds.

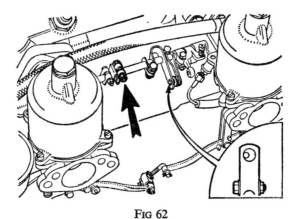

FIG 62
On multiple H type layouts the lever and link pin
are adjusted as shown

On both types, the next step is to reconnect the choke linkage and make the necessary adjustments so that all jets commence to move simultaneously. The choke control cable is reconnected and then set so that the choke knob can be pulled out $\frac{1}{16}$in before the choke mechanism begins to move at the carburettors. As on the single carburettor, the choke knob is pulled out to the point where the jets are about to move, the engine started, and the fast idling set with the fast-idle screws (not the throttle adjusting screws, which have already been set) and the intake hiss of each carburettor is checked with the flexible tube to balance the carburettors. There are slight differences between the choke linkage of H and HS type carburettors, but the sequence of operations is the same. You should now have a set of perfectly balanced carburettors which give a smooth tick-over, clean pick-up and more-or-less instant response to the throttle.

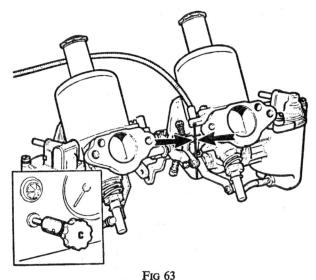

FIG 63
Fast-idle adjustment on twin HS types

Up to now it has been assumed that the carburettors are in good shape and that the needle moves freely in the jet. But if the piston drop-test shows there is some sticking of the needle, some re-adjustment is needed.

Jet Centring

Again we come up against a slightly different jet assembly and choke linkage on the H and HS types, so they will be dealt with separately.

HS Types Release the jet control link from the plastic mount-

ing block at the bottom of the jet, undo the union that secures
the flexible feed pipe to the base of the float chamber, and withdraw the jet. Now remove the jet locking spring and adjusting
nut (see diagram) and replace the jet, inserting the fuel feed
pipe connection into the float chamber. Slacken the jet locking
nut until the assembly is free to rotate.

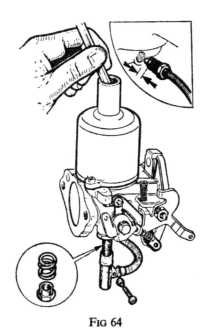

FIG 64

When centring the jet on HS carburettors, the
flexible pipe is disconnected at the float chamber

At the top of the carburettor, remove the damper and, using
a pencil, apply pressure to the top of the piston rod, at the same
time maintaining some upward pressure on the plastic end of
the jet. Tighten the jet locking nut. Finally, check for smooth
movement of the piston, using the lifting pin. Re-fit the jet locking spring and adjusting nut. Before replacing the fuel feed pipe
in the float chamber base, fit the rubber sealing washer over
the end of the plastic pipe so that at least $\frac{3}{32}$in of pipe pro-

trudes. Reassemble the controls and top up the damper with the recommended grade of oil.

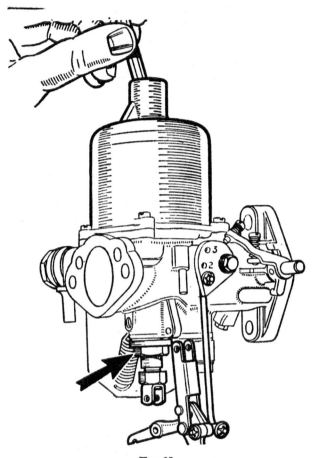

FIG 65

There is little dismantling required to centre the jet on the
H type

H Types The procedure is not quite so complicated. Again, uncouple the jet control linkage and swing it aside, mark the jet for correct reassembly, then withdraw it. Unscrew the jet adjusting nut, take off the jet locking spring, then replace the jet adjusting nut, screwing it up as far as it will go. Replace the jet, keeping its slot in line with the linkage, then slacken the jet locking nut until the assembly is free to rotate. From this point on, the procedure with the pencil and re-tightening the jet locking nut is the same as with the HS type. Check as before and reassemble the linkage.

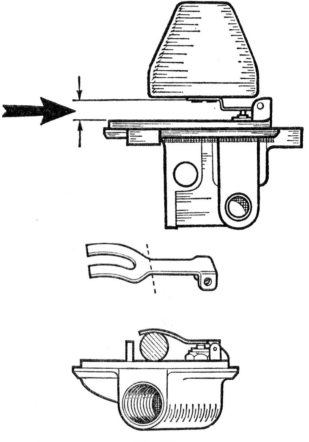

FIG 66

Fuel level is set on H types by adjusting the fork in the float chamber top until it just rests in a $\frac{7}{16}$in bar. On HS carburettors the nylon float lever is bent until there is a gap of between $\frac{1}{8}$in and $\frac{3}{16}$in at the point arrowed

Fuel Level Fuel level in the float chamber is controlled by altering the height at which the float shuts off the needle valve in the float chamber lid. The float system on H and HS type carburettors varies, and the methods of setting the correct fuel levels are shown in the diagrams.

Needle Position This can be checked when the piston/suction chamber assembly is removed. The needle type is stamped on the shank and this can be checked after loosening the clamping screw and pulling the needle out. When re-fitting, make sure that the shoulder of the shank is flush with the piston base. If you suspect a needle is bent, this can be visually checked by rotating the piston in the suction chamber. Bent ones must be renewed.

Cleaning From time to time the inside of the suction chamber and the piston should be cleaned, using a petrol-moistened cloth. There should be a small clearance between the piston edge and the chamber wall, and it is important that these components are reassembled dry, since oiling the assembly will slow down the lift of the piston. The piston rod, however, should be lightly oiled on reassembly.

Stromberg CD Carburettors

The diagrams show the similarity between the Stromberg CD carburettor and the SU. Like the SU, the two principal adjustments involve setting a throttle adjusting screw, and adjusting the height of the jet in which the needle operates, and it is important that the needle moves freely in the jet.

To tune a single Stromberg, first warm up the engine, then remove the air cleaner and the damper and use a pencil to hold the air valve hard down on the jet bridge. Now screw up the jet adjusting screw—it usually has a slotted head and a coin is ideal for turning it—until the jet is felt to come up against the

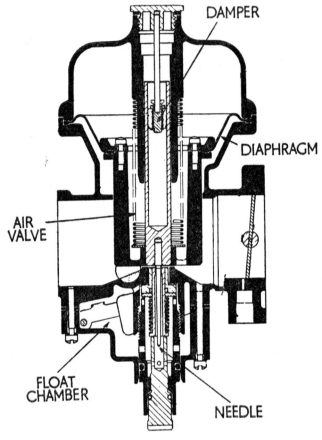

FIG 67

Cutaway of a Stromberg CD. Instead of a piston, it uses a diaphragm to lift the needle in the jet. The float chamber surrounds the jet assembly

underside of the air valve. From this position, unscrew the jet adjusting screw three turns.

Now move the throttle adjusting screw until an idling speed of about 500–650rpm is obtained. The jet adjusting screw is then screwed up to weaken, or down to richen the mixture, until the best idling speed is obtained. The correct mixture can be checked by lifting the air valve by about $\frac{1}{32}$in, using a thin screwdriver blade or using the lifting pin. As with the SU, speeding up of the engine indicates a rich mixture, a weak mixture is indicated if the engine stalls, while a similar idling speed shows that the mixture is correct.

Multiple Stromberg CDs Warm up the engine and loosen the clamping bolts on the coupling spindles between the carburettors. Loosen the throttle adjusting screws until the throttles close completely, then turn them down until they just contact the castings. From this point, tighten each one $1\frac{1}{2}$ complete turns. When this has been done check that the fast-idle screw on each carburettor is clear of the cam.

As with the single carburettor, tighten each jet adjusting screw until it meets the air valve, then unscrew it three complete turns. Check that the choke linkage is fully off with the dashboard knob pushed in. Start the engine and use a flexible tube to listen to the intake hiss on each carburettor, as detailed in the multiple SU section. Turn the throttle adjusting screws until all carburettors are balanced and a smooth idle in the correct speed range is obtained, then tighten the clamping bolts on the throttle linkage. There is no free movement as on SUs.

Mixture adjustment is now made by turning the jet adjusting screws, moving each one a similar amount, until even idling is obtained. Idling is checked by lifting each air valve $\frac{1}{32}$in with a thin screwdriver and noting the effect on idling. Make adjustments to each carburettor as detailed in the single Stromberg section, re-checking the mixture at the other carburettors after each movement of the jet adjusting screw since there is some inter-action. The ideal situation is when any air valve can be lifted $\frac{1}{32}$in with little effect on idling speed, or a minor drop in rpm. If, after setting the mixture, the idling speed has increased, reduce it by unscrewing all throttle adjusting screws by the same amount.

When the carburettors have been adjusted, the fast-idle setting on the choke linkage should be checked. Unfortunately, there is no overall setting for this and the appropriate gap between

M

the fast-idle screw head and the cam should be given in the
tuning kit fitting instructions. As a rule of thumb, if there are
no instructions, start with a $\frac{1}{32}$in gap and check its effect on the
next cold start. If the engine stalls when idling cold, close the
gap a little, if the engine speed is too fast, open up the gap.
Tighten the lock-nut securely each time and always ensure that
there is *some* gap at the end of the fast-idle screw when the choke
is out of action.

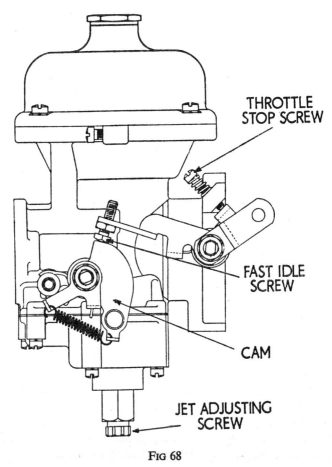

THROTTLE
STOP SCREW

FAST IDLE
SCREW

CAM

JET ADJUSTING
SCREW

Fig 68

External adjustments on the Stromberg CD

Jet Centring Take off the air cleaner and lift the air valve with a screwdriver. Screw up the jet adjusting screw until the top of the jet is just above the bridge. Slacken the jet assembly hexagon about half a turn. Allow the air valve to fall—if necessary, help it on its way by pushing it down with a pencil from the top after removing the damper. The needle will centralise the jet. Now slowly tighten the hexagon on the jet assembly, checking from time to time that the needle is still falling freely.

Fuel Level Stromberg carburettors have different fuel level settings depending on the installation. The measurement is taken with the carburettor inverted and is the distance between the face of the main body of the carburettor and the highest point of the twin floats. Adjustment is made by bending the tab which bears on the float chamber needle valve, although for small drops in fuel level Zenith recommends that a packing washer is put under the needle valve assembly.

Needle Position Stromberg needles are shouldered like the SU, and the shoulder should be flush with the base of the air valve.

Cleaning The air valve is a fairly close fit in its bore in the choke tube and will stick if it becomes coated with excess carbon or dirt. To remove it, undo the screws securing the top cover and lift off the cover, after which the air valve assembly with diaphragm can be lifted out. The air valve and its bore can be cleaned with paraffin or petrol-moistened rag, but if it is necessary to clean the diaphragm use only a clean cloth. It is fairly common for the diaphragm to expand when removed from its housing, and this is caused by petrol on the underside. Once it has been allowed to dry, the diaphragm will revert to its original size. On re-fitting the diaphragm and air valve, make sure that the tab moulded into the diaphragm edge locates in the small recess machined in the carburettor body. The outer edge of the diaphragm has a bead moulded into it, and this should be located accurately into the groove in the carburettor body. The top cover can now be fitted. Try to line up the mounting holes accurately before putting the cover into position since this will avoid disturbing the properly located diaphragm.

Fish Carburettors

Compared with production-line carburettors, the Fish is something of a special case. It is made in Britain in small numbers by two companies and is known as the Minnow-Fish or the Reece-Fish. Both are tuned in the same way and although the Reece-Fish is illustrated in the diagram, the internals of the Minnow-Fish are almost identical, so the tuning data applies to both. Fish carburettors are normally only fitted singly to road-going cars.

Like all other carburettors, the Fish has a throttle adjusting screw, but it has an air bleed screw as well, and it is the combination of these which is used to set the idling speed. As far as setting the mixture goes, there are two more adjustments—one for part-throttle, and one for full throttle running. To set the part-throttle mixture, you need a vacuum gauge. There may be a pick-up point on the carburettor for one, but if there is not, a tapping can be made into the inlet manifold as described in Chapter 6. After the engine has been warmed up, the air bleed screw is fully closed and the idling speed is set to about 2,000rpm by tightening the throttle adjusting (or stop) screw.

You now need an Allen key to fit the screw which clamps the throttle butterfly to its spindle. Using the key, loosen the screw a little until the butterfly can be moved while the spindle stays still. Move the butterfly slowly since a sudden large movement will allow the engine to gulp in too much air and it will stall. You will then have to guess the position of the butterfly, reclamp it, and start from the beginning again.

With the butterfly loose on the spindle, move it a little in each direction until the vacuum gauge shows its highest reading.

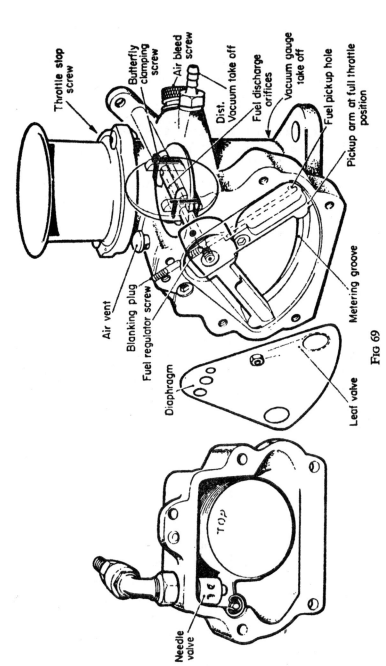

Throttle stop screw

Butterfly clamping screw

Air bleed screw

Dist. Vacuum take off

Fuel discharge orifices

Vacuum gauge take off

Fuel pickup hole

Pickup arm at full throttle position

Air vent

Blanking plug

Fuel regulator screw

Diaphragm

Leaf valve

Metering groove

Needle valve

TOP

FIG 69

Filleted Fish: the internals of the Reece-Fish carburettor

Clamp it in this position. The part-throttle mixture is now set, and the engine can be re-tuned to its idling speed and the air bleed re-set.

To set the full-throttle mixture, you need either a roller-brake dynamometer or a stretch of empty road with a couple of landmarks. The same Allen key that fitted the throttle screws also fits the blanking plug in the carburettor body just above the pick-up arm pivot. Remove this plug and pull the throttle linkage to give the full-throttle position. You will see under the plug another Allen screw—the fuel regulator screw used to set the full-throttle mixture.

On a roller brake dynamometer, the car sits with its driving wheels in the rollers which are loaded up so that it requires full throttle to operate at, say, 4,000rpm. In the middle of all this din, a carburettor tuner adjusts the fuel regulator screw and watches the tachometer for a slight improvement in engine rpm. The correct setting is the one which gives maximum revs. On the road, making the same adjustment is less hectic but takes more time. The car is driven past a landmark at, say, 40mph in top gear, and the accelerator pressed to the floorboards. When the speed gets to around 60mph, look for another landmark and note the speed as the car goes past.

Now adjust the fuel regulator screw one flat of the Allen key in a clockwise direction. This will weaken the full-throttle mixture. Try the test again, and if there is an improvement in speed at the second landmark, you are moving the screw in the right direction. Continue weakening the mixture, making a note of the number of flats you turn the screw, until performance begins to drop off. Now back off the screw to the setting that gave the highest speed. If your first one or two adjustments gave a poorer performance, you were turning the screw the wrong way, and the mixture should be richened. If this is the case, return the screw to its starting position and then turn it one flat anti-clockwise, continuing in this direction until the best speed is obtained.

Once it is set, the Fish carburettor rarely needs much attention. A helpful feature is the float chamber level plug which can be removed to check the fuel level (it should be fractionally below the hole) without first having to dismantle the float chamber.

Fixed-choke Carburettors

In this category come the Weber, Dellorto, Nikki, Solex and Zenith carburettors. Frankly, once the jets have been set on these, there's little that can be done other than set the idling. About the only worthwhile test would be to obtain one or two alternative main or air correction jets and experiment systematically checking the results against a stop-watch. Bear in mind that a larger air-correction jet weakens the mixture—especially at high rpm. Setting the idle is normally a matter of adjusting the throttle adjusting screw to give a slow tick-over and then adjusting the volume control screw—which bleeds a stream of petrol into the choke tube on the engine side of the throttle butterfly—to give the smoothest running. The throttle adjusting screw is then used to re-set the speed of idling.

Ignition Timing The method of road-testing used to set the full-throttle mixture on the Fish carburettor can also be used to set-up the ignition timing to best suit your engine and the fuel it is using. Ignition-timing adjustment, however, is not quite so straightforward as carburettor adjustment. For instance, it is possible to advance the ignition timing so that a useful power increase is obtained at high rpm. This is known as power tuning, and although it sounds a pretty useful way of doing things, on a standard engine, power-tuning may cause over-advancing of the ignition—which can have such disastrous effects as causing holes to appear in pistons. To avoid this, any ignition timing adjustment is best done over a fairly wide range of engine speeds. In this way you end up with a reasonable compromise without the risk of doing permanent internal damage.

Bearing this in mind, the car should be accelerated from fairly low down in the rev-range—say, from 30mph in top to about 60mph, comparing the speeds at two landmarks as before. The ignition timing is then altered either by turning the vernier on the side of the distributor, or by slackening the distributor clamp bolt and turning the complete unit. Turning the distributor against the rotation of the rotor arm advances the ignition, turning it the other way retards it. As with the Fish tuning, make one or two runs to make sure you are turning the vernier or distributor in the right direction, and keep a note of the amount of movement and the result. The best speed of course, is the most favourable setting.

Misfiring A misfire at high engine revolutions can be one of the most difficult faults to iron out, particularly since it often disappears as soon as the revs drop a little. Most people suspect the spark plugs when this happens, but it is often difficult to tell which cylinder is giving the trouble, particularly if all the cylinders are firing properly at idling speed. One way of checking is to run the car at the speed at which the misfire occurs, and cut the ignition while the engine is misfiring. The engine cut-out must be clean and the best way of doing this is to switch off the ignition and push down the clutch simultaneously, then knock the car out of gear and coast to a halt. You then have to remove the plugs from the engine (remember they will be very hot) and examine the insulator nose on each one. The plug from the cylinder that is misfiring will have a blacker deposit on it than the rest.

The next stage is to swap this plug round with one of the 'good' plugs and do the same test again. If the same cylinder is misfiring, you know that the trouble is not due to the plug—it is somewhere else, possibly the HT lead leaking to earth somewhere, or a bad connection on the HT side.

Carburettor Settings

SU Carburettors

Car	Year	SU type		Needle		Spring
			rich	s td	weak	colour
AUSTIN						
Healey Sprite Mk1	1959	pair H1	EB	GG	MOW	
Healey 3000 BN1	1959	pair HD6	RD	CV	SQ	yellow
Mini 848cc	1959	single HS2	M	EB	GG	red
Mini-Cooper 997cc	1961/2	pair HS2	AH2	GZ	EB	red
A60	1961/2	single HS2	M	GX	GG	yellow
A40 Mk2	1961/2	single HS2	AH2	M	EB	red
Healey Sprite II (948cc)	1961/2	pair HS2	V2	V3	GX	blue
Healey Sprite II (1098cc)	1962/3	pair HS2	M	GY	GG	blue
Healey Sprite III (1098cc)	1963/4	pair HS2	H6	AN	GG	blue
Healey 3000 II	1962/3	pair HS6	RD	BC	TZ	green
A40 and 1100	1962	single HS2	H6	AN	EB	red
Cooper 'S' (970cc)	1964	pair HS2	H6	AN	EB	red
Cooper 'S' (1070cc)	1963/4	pair HS2	3	HS	EB	red
Cooper 'S' (1275cc)	1964	pair HS2	AH2	M	EB	red
Cooper 998cc	1964/70	pair HS2	M	GY	GG	blue
1800	1964	single HS6	SW	TW	CIW	yellow
Mini Auto 850cc	1965/7	single HS4	H6	AN	EB	red
1100 Auto	1965/7	single HS4	BQ	DL	ED	red
Mini MkII 998cc	1967	single HS2	M	GX	GG	red
Mini MkII auto (998cc)	1967	single HS4	M1	AC	HA	red
1300	1967	single HS4	BQ	DZ	CF	red
Healey-Sprite IV (1275cc)	1967	pair HS2	H6	AN	GG	blue
MG						
1100	1962/8	pair HS2	D6	D3	GV	blue
MGB	1962/	pair HS4	6	MB	21	red
MGB and GT	1966–	pair HS4	6	5	21	red
MGC	1967/8	pair HS6	SQ	ST	CIW	yellow
For 1300 and Midget see equivalent Austin						
TRIUMPH						
TR3, TR3A, TR4	1959/62	pair H6	RH	SM	SL	red
Spitfire Mk2	1962/6	pair HS2	H6	AN	EB	red
TR4A	1965/6	pair HS6	SW	TW	CIW	red
Spitfire Gp 2 (1147cc)	1966	pair H4		DB		blue
Spitfire 3 (1296cc)	1968/70	pair HS2		BO		red

Car	Year	SU type	rich	Needle s td	weak	Spring colour
1300 TC	1968/70	pair HS2		BO		red
CONVERSIONS						
Cooper 'S' Gp 2 (970cc)		pair H4		CP4		blue
Cooper 'S' Gp 2 (1070cc)		pair H4		MME		blue
Cooper 'S' Gp 2 (1275cc)		pair H4		BG		blue
Hillman Minx (1390cc)	1956/8	pair H2	CU	CZ	CF	blue
Minx 1600	1959/61	pair H2		GR		blue
Imp	1964	pair HS4		H4		blue
Minx 1600	1964	pair H4		QA		red
Triumph Vitesse	1963/4	pair HS2		MO		red

Stromberg CD Carburettors

Car	CD type	Needle	Spring colour
BMC			
Mini 850cc	or single 125 CD	5A	blue*
	single 150 CD	15X	natural
Austin/Morris1100			
Austin A40	single 125 CD	5B	natural
Morris Minor 1098cc			
Sprite Mk2/Midget 948cc	pair 125 CD	6C	natural
Austin A55			
Morris Oxford Series V			
Wolseley 15/60	single 125 CD	5E	natural
Austin A40 MkII, 948cc			
Morris Minor 948cc			
Austin A60			
Morris Oxford VI	single 125 CD	5D	natural
Wolseley 16/60			
FORD			
Anglia 105E 997cc			
Anglia 1200cc	single 125 CD	6T	natural
Cortina 1200cc			
Alexander 1500cc	pair 150 CD	7A	blue*
Marcos-Ford 1500	pair 150 CD	7C	natural
CHRYSLER-ROOTES			
Imp Sport, Chamois Sport Stiletto	pair 125 CDS	6K	natural

Car		CD type	Needle	Spring colour
Rally Imp		pair 150 CD	6F	red*
Hunter/Vogue 1725cc	1966/68	single 150 CDS	6P	red*
Hunter/Vogue 1725cc	1968/70	single 150 CDS	6Z	natural
Minx/Gazelle 1500cc and 1725cc iron head		single 150 CDS	6Q	red*
Avenger 1250cc		single 150 CDS	5BB	red*
Avenger 1500cc		single 150 CDS	6AG	red*
Sunbeam Alpine 1725cc	1966/68	pair 150 CD	5M	natural
Rapier Mk1 1725cc	1967/69	pair 150 CDS	6R	blue*
Alpine GT 1725cc	1969	pair 150 CDSE	B5AU	blue*
Alpine GT 1725cc	1969/70	pair 150 CDSE	B5BC	blue*
TRIUMPH				
1300 Herald 13/60		single 150 CD	6E	
Vitesse 1600cc	1962/5	pair 125 CD	5C	natural
Vitesse 1600cc	1965/6	pair 150 CD	7B	
Vitesse 2000cc	1966/8	pair 150 CD	6J	natural
Vitesse 2000cc	1969/70	pair 150 CDS	6AC	blue*
TR4		pair 175 CD	2A	natural
TR4A	mid-1965	pair 175 CD	2E	natural
TR4A	1965	pair 175 CD	2H	blue
TR250	1968/9	pair 175 CD-2SE	B2Y	blue
TR6	1970	pair 175 CD-2SE	B1AF	blue
2000	1964/7	pair 150 CD	7A	natural
2000	1967/8	pair 150 CD	6J	natural
2000	1970	pair 150 CDS	5AN	blue*
GT6	1968/9	pair 150 CDSE	6W	blue*
GT6	1969/70	pair 150 CDS	6AC	blue*
	or	pair 150 CDSE	B5AJ	blue*
Stag V8	1970	pair 175 CD-2S	B1AQ	blue
VAUXHALL				
Viva HA90, SL90 1057cc	1965/6	single 150 CD	6G	blue*
Viva HB90, SL90 1159cc	1966/9	single 150 CD	6N	blue*
Viva 1600cc		single 175 CD-2SE	B3F	red
Viva GT 1975cc	1968/9	pair 175 CD-2S	1C	red*
Viva GT 1975cc	1969/70	pair 175 CD-2S	1AA	red*
Victor 2000, 2000SL and Super		single 175 CD-2S	2AM	blue
VX/490 1975cc		pair 175 CD-2S	1AS	red*

* = both ends

Weber Carburettors

The following settings are used by Ford on the Weber 32 DFM progressive twin-choke carburettor fitted to the Escort GT tuned to stages 2 and 3.
Stage 2:

	Primary choke		Secondary choke
Diameter	26mm		27mm
Main jet	140		115
Air correction	120		120
Emulsion tube	F24		F6
Idling jet	50		50
Accelerator pump		50	

Stage 3:

	Primary choke		Secondary choke
Diameter	26mm		27mm
Main jet	140		130
Air correction	130		110
Emulsion tube	F24		F6
Idling jet	55		50
Accelerator pump		50	

8

CUSTOMISING

Dream cars rarely come off the production line. They are usually painstakingly built by hand by a few coachbuilders for exhibition at a few motor shows, after which the car is often sold to a wealthy enthusiast. To make the average production car look like a true dream car would take a vast sum of money and some very skilled coachbuilding—a somewhat uneconomic exercise.

Fortunately, if you are willing to stick to a few simple body modifications, it is possible to make your car look different from the others. In fact, if you modify the engine and suspension on some cars, a small amount of re-shaping is essential. We have already seen that wide wheels sometimes require flared wheel arches to conform to vehicle regulations, while a non-standard carburettor, for instance, may need a 'power bulge' in the bonnet-top before the lid can be shut down.

Reworking the body in small areas like this need not cost much, and the jobs detailed in this chapter can be finished in a weekend or two. Bearing in mind that it takes years to train a professional panel-beater, you can hardly be expected to learn the body-beating trade in time to begin work on your car next weekend. Luckily, the advent of plastic body filler and resin-bonded glass fibre has meant that you do not need to use a panel-beater's hammer at all. In fact, if you can make things in modelling clay, you can make a start on re-shaping your car. Let us first take a look at the materials involved.

Plastic Filler Plastic body filler comes in two forms, either as a ready-mixed paste to which hardener is added to make it cure, or as a powder, with hardener included, which is mixed with a resin to form a paste. Of the two, the first is the quickest and easiest to use, but it is also the more expensive. Both give the same results when they have hardened off.

When it is mixed, filler is very sticky, but it will not take to surfaces which have oil, wax or grease on them—so some surface preparation is needed. On metal bodywork it is best to scrape or abrade the paint off and file, score or drill small holes in the metal to give a 'key' for the plastic to cling to. Providing this is done, there should be no chance of the filler falling out. At normal room temperature, most filler mixes will begin to cure and stiffen-up after 10–15 minutes, so do not mix more than you can use in this time.

Normal practice is to use a little more filler than necessary so that the surplus can be rubbed down to the desired shape. In fact, it is possible to do a little rough shaping with a knife while the filler has begun to cure, but is still soft. Once it has hardened off, the most trying part of the job—the rubbing down begins. I am in favour of beginning this job with a perforated file or very coarse (100 grade) wet-or-dry abrasive paper used with plenty of water. This will allow you to get the desired shape quickly, before you lose interest and bodge the job because you have become bored. Further rubbing-down can then be done using progressively finer grade papers. From 100, use 180 grade, then 240 followed by, perhaps, 320. These grades are approximate, if they are not available, the next-nearest will do.

When you get to the 240 stage, you should be very near the final shape. Examine the filler surface for flaws. There will probably be a few craters caused by small air-bubbles. Dry the filler, mix up a new batch and wipe a thin film over the surface to fill them. Eventually, after more filling-in and rubbing down, you will obtain the desired contour.

Glass Fibre Unlike filler, which has little load-bearing strength, resin-bonded glass fibre is a material tough enough to be used for making complete car bodies. Like filler, it will readily adhere to a suitably 'keyed' metal panel and is, therefore, an ideal material for forming body additions such as air-scoops, wheel arch extensions, and for fairing-in extra lamps.

Unfortunately, in its cured state, it is not so easily smoothed down as filler. So, for glass fibre additions that are on view, it is preferable to use a female mould, so that the end product has a smooth outer surface. The method of making a mould and casting from it is explained in the section of this chapter dealing with headlamp fairings.

The backbone of all resin-bonded glass fibre is the glass mat, and the most common type used in automobile work is chopped strand mat where the fibres are simply laid on each other at random and have no particular weave. This sort of mat will readily take up compound curved shapes and is the best for moulding. It is also useable on flat surfaces, although here, if you have some other sort of glass fibre woven mat, for instance, or even old glass fibre curtains—you can use these instead.

The glass cloth is impregnated by resin which is mixed with hardener in small batches in the same way as filler. The best way to apply resin is with a cheap paint brush, using a stippling action to get all the air bubbles out. Glass fibre specialists can supply a brush cleaner which will prevent the brush from 'curing' in the interval between the lay-up of laminations. This only works if the brush is immersed while the resin is still soft. Once it is hardened, the brush is useless. If you do not have any resin solvent, methylated spirit or cellulose thinners will keep it relatively soft, but make sure the bristles are wiped with a cloth until they are almost dry before using it in a fresh batch of resin.

Painting

Most popular cars are painted with a synthetic alkyd high-bake enamel, which is sprayed on and then oven-baked to cure it. Alternatively, the car may be sprayed in acrylic paint and then heat-treated to partially melt the surface and cause it to flow slightly and produce a shiny, smooth surface.

With the exception of small articles which you could conceivably put in the domestic oven, heat-treatment is not possible for 'do-it-yourself' painting, and the alternative is an air-drying cellulose.

Since cars come from the factory spray-painted, the best method of matching the existing paint is to spray the new paint on. There are several alternatives here.

The easiest method is to use an aerosol can of paint which is normally readily available from motor accessory stores, each can of paint being colour-matched to blend with a manufacturer's colour. For small jobs, aerosol paint spray cans offer a cheap method of getting a pretty good finish. But they have their disadvantages. The main snag, if you are tackling a big area, is cost. Paint from an aerosol can is thinned to almost water-like consistency, and a large number of coats are needed to give a good depth of colour, particularly on lighter shades. Another problem is that, as the can empties, it will only produce a constant spray if held vertically—a point well worth remembering if you are contemplating spraying a roof. Finally, as the can empties there is usually some spluttering—and resultant blobs of paint—from the spray head, and this should be allowed for.

The next stage up from the aerosol paint can is a vibrator-type spray gun. This looks at a glance somewhat similar to the gun the professional spray painters use, but instead of having a powerful compressor to provide the air pressure needed to force the paint through the nozzle, the vibrator gun carries its own electric air pump in the head.

There are several types available priced up to about £15, and they have the obvious advantage over the aerosol that you can buy your own paint separately, and, therefore, more cheaply. But like aerosols, they have small nozzles and the paint must be thinned—usually at least 60 per cent thinners is needed to 40 per cent paint. With these guns it is possible to reduce the proportion of thinners—and therefore to give fewer coats—if the paint is warmed a little before being sprayed. The best way to do this is to attach an extension pick-up tube to the gun (a length of pvc tube is ideal) and use a remote paint container standing in a large bowl of hot water. Since cellulose is highly inflammable, obviously it must never be heated by a naked flame or element. The ideal water temperature will depend on the proportion of thinners used and the make of vibrator gun, and if you are tackling a large area, as the water in the outer container cools it will have to be drained off and topped-up with more hot water. A wife with a constantly steaming kettle can be helpful at times like these.

At the top of the tree in the re-spraying business is a paint spray gun and separate compressor. Small spray outfits like this can be had for around £25, which is expensive if you only want to treat one car, although if you anticipate doing a lot of spray work, a compressor and spray gun will give the best job for the least effort.

The area you paint and the way the paint is sprayed on will have a marked effect on the appearance of the finished job. It is very difficult exactly to match new paint with old, simply because weathering will have slightly changed the colour of the old paint. Therefore, to disguise any slight mis-match, it is best when spraying a small area to take the edge of the new paint up to a natural join-line on the car. This means, for instance, that even when spraying a small reshaped section on the bonnet, the complete bonnet should be painted.

When putting on paint with a spray gun or aerosol, the area should be sprayed in a series of horizontal lines, starting from the top and stopping the spray and re-starting it at the end of each stroke. If the spray is not shut off at the point where the

N

gun changes direction, the over-spray will give the ends a double thickness of paint and it will probably run. The distance between the nozzle and the surface to be painted depends on the delivery rate. As a rough guide, if the nozzle is too close the rapid build-up of paint will cause runs, whereas if the nozzle is too distant the paint droplets will partially dry *en route* and the surface will be rough, with no gloss. The above conditions also apply in the same order if the paint is too thin or too thick. In fact, if you are not familiar with spray painting it is worth while having a practice on an old sheet of metal or wood—even a cardboard carton—before starting on the car.

It is not generally realised that the colour coat is not completely waterproof, so to prevent rust from forming under it later it is essential to apply several coats of primer to any bare metal.

There are several types of primer, some of them containing rust inhibitors, but the most useful is called primer-surfacer, which, besides adding a waterproof coating, also fills any small imperfections. It will not, however, fill big indentations, and for those that are too small to be treated with plastic filler but too big for primer-surfacer to fill, cellulose stopper—a grey paste-like material—can be put on with a knife-blade. Stopper, unlike plastic filler, does not harden quickly if put on in large quantities. The secret of success is to apply it in very thin layers. It should be left overnight to harden, before rubbing-down.

Adding Louvres

Some performance cars are made with their bonnet-tops perforated with louvres which keep down the temperature in the engine bay. On cars where the engine has been reworked to improve its power output, the same rule sometimes applies, and there are available louvre panels which can be grafted on to a reasonably flat surface quite easily.

The job obviously involves cutting a hole in the bonnet top. This may sound drastic, but approached properly the task of cutting an aperture in otherwise sound bodywork need not cause difficulty. The tidiest method is to use a sheet metal 'nibbler' like the Monodex cutter illustrated on p 152. Although it can go round corners, it is less likely to break its blade if kept in a straight line. The method to use when cutting an oblong hole is to drill a ¼in hole at each corner and then join them up with the cutter.

Fig 70

First drill four holes—the first stage in cutting the oblong hole in a bonnet-top to fit a louvre panel. A paper template has been taped on to indicate the shape required

If you do not want to buy or hire a 'nibbler', a padsaw with a metal-cutting blade will do a satisfactory job, although it will probably take longer. The longest method of all is to drill a series of holes very close together around the edge, and gently merge them into one long slot using a very sharp cold chisel and a 2lb hammer.

Once you have sorted out how you are going to cut the hole, the rest is easy. The quickest way to fix the louvre panels in place is, of course, to blind-rivet them directly over the hole. This is effective but looks clumsy and amateurish. It is better to take more time and make the louvres appear part of the original coachwork.

In order to do this, besides the louvre panels you will need about 1lb of plastic body filler, some strips of glass fibre tape and resin and a reel of self-adhesive tape.

First of all, using a sharp corner as a form, bend down the metal at each side of the panel, leaving about ¼in between the bend and the edge of the louvres. Now mark the shape of this panel on the bonnet-top. You can either scribe it on the paint, or make up a template and tape it in place, but before finally deciding on its position, check under the bonnet in case you are fouling any cross-members. It is much easier if you avoid these.

Once the hole has been cut, file the edges until the panel fits it accurately. If the bonnet is curved, use tin-snips to cut a series of slits in the turned-down edges. These will allow the panel to be bent so that it conforms to the body shape.

The next stage is to 'tack' the panel in position, using body filler. But before this goes on, the edges of the hole should be roughed-up with a coarse file or carborundum paper to give the filler a satisfactory 'key'. An area about 1in from the edge of the hole should be treated in this way, both underneath and on top.

The louvre panel can now be positioned, retaining it with sticky tape on the top side of the bonnet. Next, the filler can go on. Turn the bonnet upside-down and work filler round the edge of the panel, tamping it into the join line. When the filler

Fig 71

Held by adhesive tape on top, the underside of the louvre panel is temporarily fixed using plastic filler paste

has set, a hack-saw blade can be used to trim off the surplus metal from the bent-down section.

The panel is now permanently fixed using resin-bonded glass fibre. If you do not have 1in wide glass tape, the more common chopped-strand mat, cut into strips, will do. The only advantage of tape here is that it gives a smoother finish.

Once the glass fibre has cured, work switches to the top side of the bonnet. Remove the self-adhesive tape and apply a smooth coat of filler round the edge of the panel to obliterate the join line. Blend the new metal into the bonnet beginning with about 120 grade wet-or-dry carborundum paper dipped regularly in water, and gradually use a finer grade as the job progresses. To avoid waves in the surface, the abrasive paper should be wrapped round a flat block of wood which will act

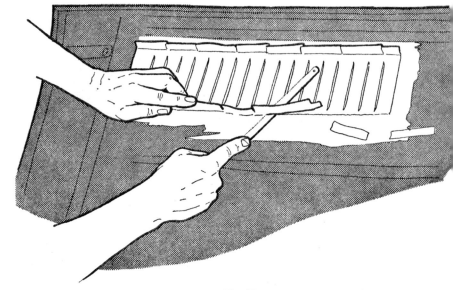

Fig 72

When the filler has hardened, a hacksaw blade cuts off the turned-down
edges of the louvre panel

like a smoothing plane and flatten out the bumps in the filler.

Most louvres are made from soft aluminium, and technically
the correct way to paint them is to use a two-part etch primer
and activator which will make subsequent coats of paint adhere
properly. Unfortunately, two-part etch primers are not normally sold in quantities of less than half a gallon of each part—
far too much to treat two small louvre panels. As an alternative,
I have found that Bondaprimer, a one-part etch primer which
is mainly intended as a rust-preventative on steel bodywork,
does a good job. Before using it, the aluminium should be
degreased by wiping it with a cloth dipped in white spirit or
methylated spirit. The primer should be left 48 hours to cure
after which it should be 'thumbnail tested'. If your thumbnail
leaves a small indent, it is not quite dry and should be left a
little longer. Once it is dry, give a coat of primer-surfacer and
four-or-five coats of top-coat to blend with the rest of the finish.

Adding Extra Lamps

Extra lamps are essential on a rally car and extremely useful on road cars in dirty weather. But one of the snags when attaching an extra light to the front of a car is that, without a very substantial mounting bracket, it can be difficult to prevent the lamp from vibrating and giving an uncertain light. There is another consideration, too: bolt-on lamps can just as easily be unbolted by thieves. One answer to both these situations is to build-in the extra lamps to the car body, and this is what was done with the Mini shown in the illustration on p 49.

The job was carried out using glass-fibre mountings for the lamps, the mountings being bonded to the bonnet-top. To preserve as much as possible the low profile of the Mini bonnet, the lamps were sunk into it, and the top edges only rise $1\frac{1}{2}$ inches above the normal bonnet line.

The lamps used were two main-beam headlamp units from a Triumph 2000. It is not essential to use lamps from this car, however, and $5\frac{3}{4}$in diameter main-beam lamps from a variety of four-headlamp cars—the overhead-camshaft Vauxhall Victor range, Triumph Vitesse, Austin 3 litre and Rover 2000, for instance—can all be used. And the cheapest way of getting hold of them is at a breaker's yard.

Once the position of the lamps had been fixed, part of the cross-bracing under the bonnet had to be cut away to make room for the mountings. The bracing pieces in this case are only spot-welded at each end, so that it is not too difficult to cut a section out using a metal nibbler and a pair of tin-snips. Before this was done, the curve of the bonnet-top was cut on a card template. The reason for this is that when the stiffeners are cut, there is a tendency for the bonnet to 'uncurl' and change its shape a little. It is important that the correct curvature is set—if necessary by bending the bonnet a little more—before the glass-fibre lamp mountings are grafted in. For if they are fitted and the curve of the bonnet is wrong, the bonnet-top will not fit, and bending it will damage the mountings. On the finished job, the addition of the mountings compensates for the missing stiffeners.

One of the problems you face when sinking two lamps into a piece of curved metal is where to start, for it is not immediately apparent where, or how big, the first hole in the metal should be. The size and position of the holes were eventually decided after making a mock-up. First a plywood ring, with an outside diameter the same as the maximum diameter of the lamp assembly, was cut out. The ring was used to help form a stiff paper tube, and the end of the tube was tailored so that it fitted snugly on the curve at the front of the bonnet with the rest of the tube horizontal. Drawing round the tailored end of the tube then gave the size of the hole required. This was then cut out using a metal nibbler.

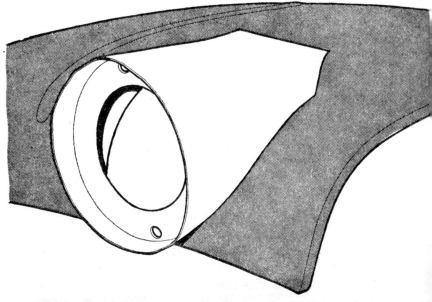

Fig 73

A paper tube attached to a former is used to mark the size of hole required in the bonnet

The plywood ring was then again used as a former. This time a sheet of soft aluminium was curved and attached to the outside of the ring, using plastic filler so that it formed a sort of tunnel ahead of it. It is easier to get a regular shape when bending aluminium if a former, such as a tin can, is used. In this case, a tin about 3in smaller in diameter than the curve required was used. This allowed the aluminium to spring a little, and grip the plywood former.

The next step involved some simple woodwork. Because the front cross-member above the Mini grille gets in the way, it is

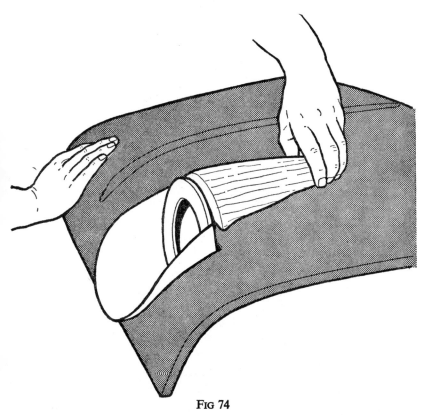

FIG 74

Basic essentials for making the master—a plywood former, aluminium extension and a wooden fairing

o

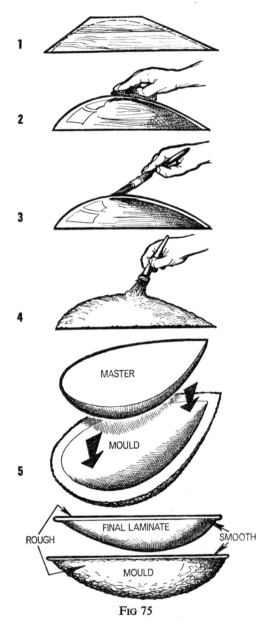

FIG 75

The five main stages of glass fibre moulding. A master is roughly shaped
from timber or plaster (1). After finishing, it is coated with parting agent
(2), then a resin gel coat (3), followed by two or three laminations of glass
mat (4). When the mould is parted from the master (5) it has a smooth
inside surface and from this the final product is cast

not possible to sink the lamps completely into the bonnet, so a small fairing was needed to blend in the 1½in or so that protruded above the top surface.

The fairing can be made from something like plaster of paris or (as in this instance) formed from a block of timber, using a small plane and sandpaper to get the desired shape. When this had been done, the plywood ring and its aluminium extension was dropped into place, aligned in the straight-ahead position, the fairing added behind it, and the whole assembly fixed together and to the metalwork with plastic filler.

This structure on the bonnet-top formed the framework of a 'master' for a mould. The mould was made from glass fibre, and from it two headlamp mountings, also in glass fibre, were cast.

It may seem a trifle long-winded to make a master, then make a mould, and then, from the mould make a couple of glass fibre castings, but there are reasons. The main one is that in this case identical headlamp mountings can be used for both the nearside and offside lamps, and the best way of making sure these *are* identical is to take them from the same mould. Secondly, the easiest way to get a smooth surface on glass fibre is to lay-up the laminate in a smooth female mould. And, lastly, although it is possible to sand down the uneven surface of chopped strand mat until it is smooth, this is a very laborious job and, where two identical shapes are involved, it is all too easy to sand down one more than the other so that they are no longer identical.

The method which is detailed here is fairly standard practice whether you are moulding a headlamp mounting or a complete car body. The main idea is to make sure that the outer surface (or the one which shows) of the end product is perfectly smooth. There is, of course, one important rule to follow when making a mould—it should be shaped so that the article being moulded can be got out reasonably easily once it has cured. This means designing a mould on the principle that if you turned it upside down, the material inside would fall out of its own accord. If

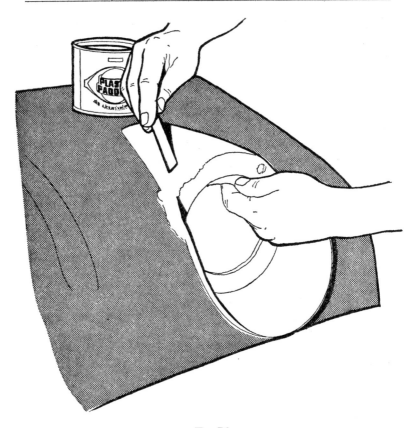

Fig 76
Filler goes on the timber to mask any wood-grain effect

this cannot be achieved—as when moulding a sphere, for instance—then two moulds are needed and the resulting two castings must be joined together.

On the Mini, the basic master for the mould was in a fairly crude state, and to smooth off some of the rough edges, filler was used. In fact, on this job I finished up coating all of the softwood sections with filler in order to avoid a wood-grain effect.

Once the correct shape had been achieved, the surface was rubbed down with progressively finer grades of wet-or-dry

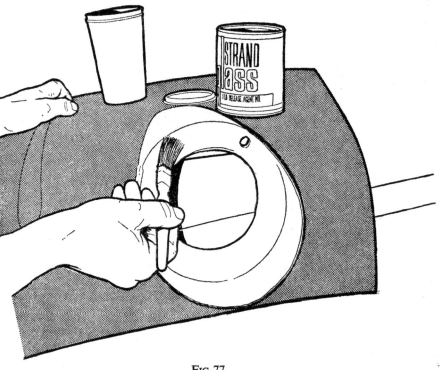

FIG 77
On goes a coat of release agent/sealer

paper, until all blemishes had been smoothed out. It was then given a coat of release agent/sealer. This material, called release agent no 1, is made by Strand Glass, which specialises in supplying glass fibre and all associated bits and pieces for 'do-it-yourself' use. Release agent no 1 dries in minutes and can be smoothed with very fine (400 grade) wet-or-dry paper, used wet, to remove any brush marks. Once a smooth surface has been obtained, release agent no 2—which does not contain any sealer—can be applied. To avoid brush marks which would be transferred to the mould, this is best wiped on with a soft cloth or a piece of tissue.

Once the master is as perfect as it can be made a 'gel' coat

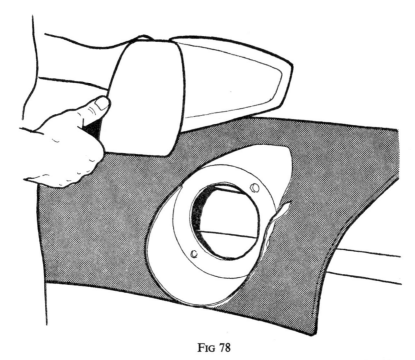

Fig 78

Parting the mould from the master—note the slight damage caused to the
master by the screwdrivers used to 'persuade' the mould to free off

of resin is brushed on. This will form the smooth inside surface
of the mould and is a trifle thicker than the resin used for
laminating glass cloth. The gel coat should be allowed to cure
before moving to the next stage, which is to apply a coat of
laminating resin and lay on the glass mat. More resin is brushed
into the mat, using a stippling action to work out any air
bubbles. For most bodywork modifications, two laminations of
chopped strand mat are normally sufficient, although, for a
small mould, it is worth while making three laminations to give
maximum stiffness, with more laminations still on a big mould.

Once the resin has cured the mould can be parted from the
master. Depending on the shape and the correct application of
parting agent, this will be an easy job or a lengthy one. It is

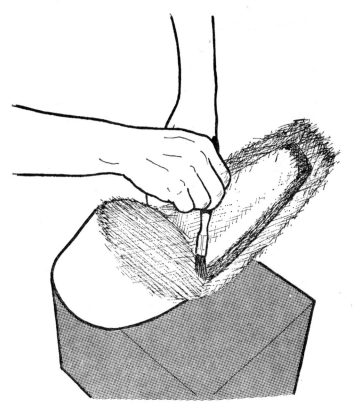

FIG 79

The first lamination of the eventual lamp mounting is laid up

customary to lay up a little extra glass fibre around the edge of
a mould to give a purchase point for a screwdriver blade and
other implements of persuasion during the parting process. Once
the mould has been separated, the smooth surface should be
checked for flaws, and where these are small ones they can be
plugged with filler. Providing the mould is satisfactory, the
master can now be destroyed.

The next stage is really a repetition of the mould-making
process. The smooth side of the mould is coated with parting
agent, then gel coat, and then two laminations are laid up.

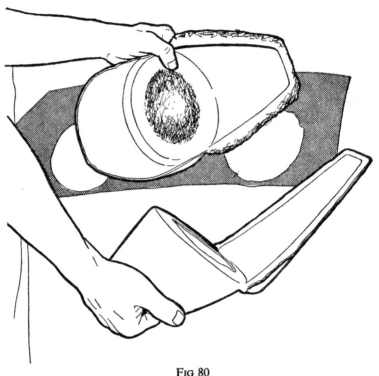

Fig 80
Start of the production line: the first lamp mounting is parted from the
mould

Leave it to cure, part it from the mould and you have your first
lamp mounting.

The mountings are fitted into the bonnet in the same way as
used for the aluminium louvres. After checking the curvature of
the bonnet with the card template, the outline of the mounting
was cut from the bonnet-top, and then the mounting was
placed in position and bonded in place with strips of glass fibre
from underneath. On the top a small fillet of filler at the join
line blended the mounting in.

At this stage, if you fit the lamps they will protrude a little,
and since these Lucas units are not built to take snap-on rims
like the larger 7in versions, the beam-setting screws and fixing

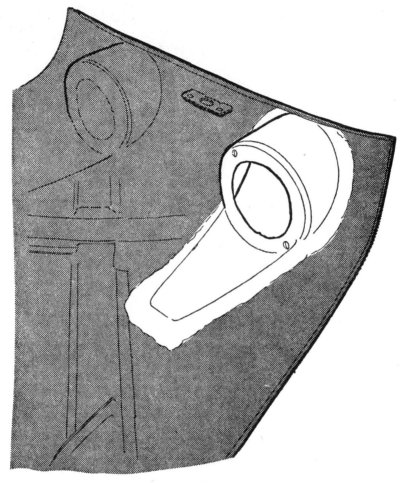

FIG 81

The side you don't see. Underneath the bonnet the lamp mounts are
secured by strips of glass fibre bonded on in the same way as the louvres
were held

pieces will be on view—not a pretty sight. The answer is to put
a hood over the top of the lamp, and this can be moulded from
a strip of flat aluminium bent to the correct radius. The resulting
laminate can be resined in place after shaping it to fit the top

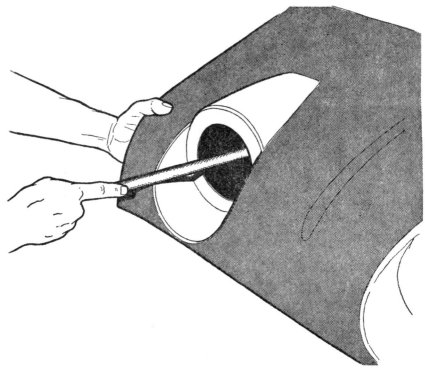

FIG 82

Cleaning-up involves tailoring the holes to suit the lamps and drilling a
number of clearance holes. Shrouds were later added on top. The final
result is shown in the illustration on p 49

curve exactly. Any small imperfections are smoothed out with
filler. Incidentally, it is not necessary to use parting agent on
the aluminium.

In this instance painting was carried out using aerosol spray
cans. First the bonnet-top—which had been cut back to the
bare metal—was given three coats of primer-surfacer. This was
followed by about four coats of colour.

The lamps were wired into the lighting circuit at the dip-
switch, so that they come into operation only on main beam.
When the lights are dipped the extra lamps go out, and the
normal headlamps provide the dipped beam.

Carbon Fibres

When glass-fibre bodywork is being used on a competition car, it is important to keep the structure as light as possible. With normal resin-bonded structures, this was not always easy, since thin laminates have little stiffness or strength. In fact, the bodywork of some early glass-fibre covered competition cars could be seen rippling at high speeds.

The way to stiffen-up thin laminates is to bond in carbon fibres. The fibres themselves are very like fine human hair and are sold by Strand Glass in 40in hanks. The favourite method of usage seems to be to bond in the fibres in a criss-cross pattern, with about a 1in gap between them. Unfortunately, the fibres are not cheap, but for those interested in lightness with maximum strength, they are essential.

Bolt-on Glass-fibre Panels

Although moulding your own body modifications from glass fibre is the only way to have a truly original car, for those who do not relish the thought of working through the various stages of mould-making and laminating, it is possible to purchase ready-made glass fibre body parts, and various hard-tops and modified bonnets are available to fit production cars. Possibly the most radical bodywork modification available for Minis is the one-piece glass fibre nose section which, like the E-type Jaguar bonnet, is hinged at the front so that it lifts up to expose the complete engine and front suspension.

Fitting involves using a sharp cold chisel to cut away the existing front wings, the grille surround and the valance under the front bumper. The headlamps and direction indicator lamps are transferred to the plastic nose, which is then attached at its hinge-point and secured on each side at its trailing edge by over-centre catches. The whole operation can be completed in a weekend, and the conversion is understandably popular with owners of Minis suffering from badly rusting front wings.

USEFUL ADDRESSES

Engine Tuners

ENGINE TUNERS

Alexander Engineering, Thame Road, Haddenham, Buckinghamshire (most types); Allard Motor Co Ltd, 51 Upper Richmond Road, Putney, London SW 15 (F, S/chargers for most); W. B. Blydenstein, Station Works, Shepreth, near Royston, Hertfordshire (V); British Leyland Special Tuning, Abingdon-on-Thames, Berkshire; Broadspeed Ltd, Banbury Road, Southam, Leamington Spa, Warwickshire (F); Coburn Improvements, Netherhall Gardens, London NW 3 (V); VW Derrington Ltd, 159–61 London Road, Kingston-upon-Thames, Surrey (BLMC, C, F, S-T); Downton Engineering Works Ltd, Downton, Salisbury, Wiltshire (BLMC); Ford Advanced Vehicle operations, South Ockenden, Essex; Team Hartwell, Holdenhurst Road, Bournemouth, Hampshire (C); Janspeed Engineering, Southampton Road, Salisbury, Wiltshire (BLMC, C, F, S-T); Oselli Engineering, Industrial Estate, Stanton Harcourt Road, Eynsham, Oxfordshire (BLMC); Piper Engine Development Ltd, Wotton Road, Kingsnorth Industrial Estate, Ashford, Kent (most types); Race-Proved Performance & Racing Equipment, 177 Uxbridge Road, Hanwell, Middlesex (F); S.A.H. Accessories Ltd, Linslade, Leighton Buzzard, Bedfordshire (S-T, Saab); Speedwell Ltd, 260–300 Berkhamsted

Road, Chesham, Buckinghamshire (BLMC, F, VW); John Willment (Mitcham) Ltd, 189–91 Streatham Road, Mitcham, Surrey (F).

Code: BLMC = British Leyland
C = Chrysler-Rootes
F = Ford
S-T = Standard-Triumph
V = Vauxhall

CARBURETTORS

SU Carburettor Co, Erdington, Birmingham; Zenith Carburettor Co Ltd, Honeypot Lane, Stanmore, Middlesex (Stromberg CD); Fiat (England) Ltd, Great West Road, Brentford, Middlesex (Weber); Leonard Reece & Co, Beeches Avenue, Carshalton, Surrey (Fish); Minnow Fish Carburettors Ltd, Minnow House, Lochgilphead, Argyllshire (Fish); Chris Montague Carburettor Co, 364 Cricklewood Lane, London NW 2 (Weber tuning); Radbourne Ltd, 8 Bramber Road, London W 14 (Weber tuning).

BRAKES

Automotive Products Group (Lockheed), Tachbrook Road, Leamington Spa, Warwickshire; Ferodo Ltd, Chapel-en-le-Frith, Stockport, Cheshire; Girling Ltd, Kings Road, Tyseley, Birmingham 11.

SUSPENSION

Armstrong Patents Ltd, Eastgate, Beverley, Yorkshire; J. W. E. Banks Ltd, Crowland, Peterborough (Koni shock absorbers).

OIL COOLERS

Serck Services, 456 Stratford Road, Sparkhill, Birmingham.

INSTRUMENTS

AC-Delco Ltd, Dunstable, Bedfordshire; Smiths Industries Ltd, Oxgate Lane, Cricklewood, London NW 2.

LAMPS

Britover (Continental) Ltd, 387–9 Chapter Street, London NW 2 (Cibie). Joseph Lucas Ltd, Great King Street, Birmingham, 18.

ELECTRIC FANS

Kenlowe Accessories & Co Ltd, Burchetts Green, near Maidenhead, Berkshire; Wood-Jeffreys Ltd, North Road, Kirkburton, Huddersfield, Yorkshire.

GLASS FIBRE

Bondaglass Ltd, 158–64 Ravenscroft Road, Beckenham, Kent (Bondaprimer); Strand Glass Co Ltd, Brent Way Trading Estate, Brentford, Middlesex.

INDEX